LOOKING AT
ANCIENT HISTORY

R. J. UNSTEAD

AUTHOR OF 'LOOKING AT HISTORY'
'PEOPLE IN HISTORY', ETC.

NEW YORK
THE MACMILLAN COMPANY

Also by R. J. Unstead

LOOKING AT HISTORY

BOOK
1. FROM CAVEMEN TO VIKINGS
2. THE MIDDLE AGES
3. TUDORS AND STUARTS
4. QUEEN ANNE TO QUEEN ELIZABETH II

PEOPLE IN HISTORY

BOOK
1. FROM CARACTACUS TO ALFRED
2. FROM WILLIAM THE CONQUEROR TO WILLIAM CAXTON
3. GREAT TUDORS AND STUARTS
4. GREAT PEOPLE OF MODERN TIMES

ENGLAND

BOOK
1. THE MEDIEVAL SCENE
2. CROWN AND PARLIAMENT
3. THE RISE OF GREAT BRITAIN
4. A CENTURY OF CHANGE

MEN AND WOMEN IN HISTORY

BOOK
1. HEROES AND SAINTS
2. PRINCES AND REBELS
3. DISCOVERERS AND ADVENTURERS
4. GREAT LEADERS

BLACK'S JUNIOR REFERENCE BOOKS

A HISTORY OF HOUSES
TRAVEL BY ROAD
MONASTERIES

EARLY TIMES

TEACHING HISTORY IN THE JUNIOR SCHOOL

ACKNOWLEDGMENTS

The author is indebted to his wife for her assistance in gathering material for this book, and in preparing it for publication.

Most of the drawings are by J. C. B. Knight. The cover design is by Alan Sorrell. The maps are by Cyril Webber.

Grateful acknowledgement is made to the following for their permission to reproduce photographs and drawings : the Greek Government Department of Information, pages 55, 65 (a), 111 (a) ; the Trustees of the British Museum, pages 10 (c), 11 (b), 13 (a), 23, 25 (a and c), 35 (a), 45 (c), 56 (b), 59, 67 (b), 70 (a) ; the Mansell Collection, pages 26, 31, 34 (a), 36 (b), 37, 39, 44, 48, 50 (f), 57 (b), 64, 70 (b), 73 (a and b), 80 (b), 81 (a, b and c), 82 (b), 84, 87 (b), 88, 89 (b), 91 (a), 96 (a), 98, 103 (c), 104 (b), 105, 108, 109.

Acknowledgment is also made for the use of drawings on pages 6 (a), 7 (a and d), 17 (a and b), 21 (a, b and c), 35 (b), 38 (b), 42 (a), 43 (a), 45 (a and b) from *Ancient Egyptian, Mesopotamian and Persian Costume*, by Mary Houston ; pages 48 (c and d), 49 (b), 50 (a, b, c and d), 51 (b), 52 (a), 54 (a, b and c), 69 (a), 73 (c), 91 (b), 93, 94, 99, 100 (a), from *Ancient Greek, Roman and Byzantine Costume*, by Mary Houston ; pages 12 (a), 16 (b), 18 (a), 20 (a), 21 (d), from *The Story of the Pharaohs*, by James Baikie.

FIRST PUBLISHED APRIL 1959

REPRINTED 1959, 1961, 1964 AND 1966

MADE AND PRINTED IN GREAT BRITAIN BY
MORRISON AND GIBB LTD., LONDON AND EDINBURGH

CONTENTS

PART ONE : ANCIENT EGYPT

PART ONE : ANCIENT EGYPT

1. THE PHARAOHS

THE NILE VALLEY

The earliest civilizations in the world began when men had time to do more than merely struggle to keep themselves alive by hunting or gathering food.

Ancient Egypt, one of the countries in which a great civilization first arose, possessed several important advantages. The climate was very warm and the soil of the Nile Valley was very fertile. There were two reasons for this. Firstly, the great river provided ample water which could be raised and poured on to the fields by means of one of the earliest inventions in the world, the *shadoof*.

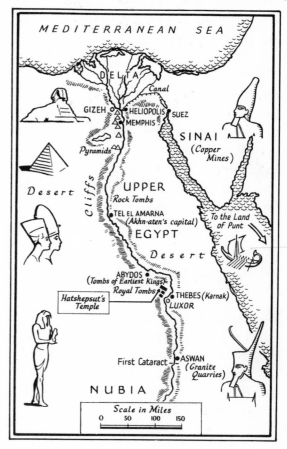

Ancient Egypt

Raising water by means of a shadoof

This was a long pole with a bucket at one end and a weight at the other.

The second reason for the great fertility of the soil was that, every year, heavy rains in Central Africa caused the Nile to overflow its banks and to spread a layer of rich mud over the fields. This annual flooding was known as the *Inundation*.

5

Egypt was protected from enemies by the deserts which stretched to east and west on either side of the river. To the north was the sea, and to the south the barrier of a great waterfall, the First Cataract.

The Nile valley was narrow, but at its mouth, where it entered the Mediterranean Sea, was a marshy plain formed of river mud, called the Nile Delta. Here, in *Lower Egypt*, civilization began about seven thousand years ago.

Three Pharaohs. The first wears the red crown of Lower Egypt, the second wears the white crown of Upper Egypt, and the third wears the combined crown of the First Union

THE FIRST UNION

There were probably many early kings of Lower Egypt. Soon, another kingdom arose, stretching from the base of the Delta up the valley to the First Cataract. It was called *Upper Egypt*.

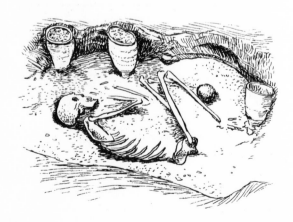

An early Egyptian grave, showing bowls for food and drink placed beside the body

After a time, a powerful king of Lower Egypt conquered his neighbour and the two kingdoms became one. This is sometimes known as the *First Union*. We know little about it, though it seems that *Heliopolis*, the Sun-City, built midway between the two kingdoms, became the first capital.

Heliopolis was always regarded as especially sacred to *Ra*, the Sun-God, greatest and most powerful of all the Egyptian gods. We know, too, that the people already believed in a life after death, for they buried their dead in shallow graves containing bowls of food and drink. They also placed implements of copper in the graves, though copper was still a precious and rare metal.

THE FIRST WRITING

An organized kingdom needed to keep records of events, taxes, messages and laws. So writing was invented. In the days of the two Kingdoms there had been picture-writing, and the next step was to draw an object—it might be a man, a bird, a tree— always in the same way, so that different persons would recognize what was meant.

A great step forward was to be able to write down *sounds*, so that words could be spelt out. Gradually the Egyptians used their picture-signs to stand for sounds. This kind of writing is called *Hieroglyphic*.

PAPYRUS

The country had a natural supply of materials for writing. The riverside reeds were pasted together in strips to make a thin sheet. On top was pasted a second sheet with the reeds running across the others at right angles. This made a strong, whitish paper, called *papyrus*, from the name of the reed. A brush-like reed was used as a pen, to be dipped in ink made from soot, water and a little vegetable gum.

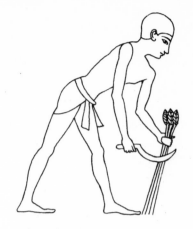

A worker harvesting papyrus

Practice helped the busy scribes to write so quickly that instead of drawing each little picture they made a sign something like it. A fellow scribe would recognize what they meant. This rapid writing was called *hieratic*, and was written from right to left, unlike our own writing. Sometimes the scribes wrote down the page instead of across.

By this time, perhaps 4,000 years before Christ was born, the Egyptians had learnt to calculate the year and to divide it into twelve months of thirty days each, with a holiday of five days to complete the year.

This is the name of an Egyptian official, written in hieroglyphics

Four Egyptian hieroglyphs

A scribe

The Great Pyramids and the Sphinx at Gizeh as they are today

THE OLD KINGDOM OR PYRAMID AGE

While these remarkable advances, and many others, were taking place, the First Union broke up and there was a period of unrest until a strong ruler emerged.

About the year 3300 B.C. (not everyone agrees about these early dates), *Menes*, ruler of Upper Egypt, conquered Lower Egypt and united the two kingdoms again. Menes was the first king, or *Pharaoh*, of the First *Dynasty*, which means a family of kings. His reign marks the beginning of the first of Egypt's three great periods. It is called the Old Kingdom or the Pyramid Age.

Early Egyptian tools

THE PYRAMIDS

The Egyptians had no large quantities of timber for building, so they used sun-baked bricks for their houses and tombs. Then the discovery of metal enabled them to make saws and tools strong enough to quarry rock. Granite and limestone from the hills bordering the Nile Valley were used to build the Pyramids.

Copper was mined in the Peninsula of Sinai, where servants of a Pharaoh of the First Dynasty carved on the mountain-side his claim to the copper mines.

About 3000 B.C., *Imhotep*, the royal architect, built the first great stone building. It was the Step Pyramid, tomb of his master, Pharaoh *Zoser*, and it is probably the oldest building in the world.

8

Building the Great Pyramid

THE GREAT PYRAMID

The Great Pyramid, largest of all the pyramids, was built at Gizeh for a Pharaoh of the Fourth Dynasty named *Khufu*, or *Cheops*. There are 2,300,000 blocks of limestone, each weighing about two and a half tons, and the pyramid, nearly 500 feet high, covers thirteen acres.

BUILDING THE PYRAMIDS

It is said that an army of 100,000 men was employed for twenty years building this great tomb. The stones were brought from the quarries in barges and hoisted ashore. Then each stone was probably levered on to a sledge, which was dragged up an earthen ramp by hundreds of workers. Water was poured in front of the sledge to help it to run easily and an overseer beat time with wooden clappers to encourage the labourers. As the pyramid rose higher, so the earth ramp was raised.

TOMB ROBBERS

In the heart of the pyramid, or underneath it, was a small burial chamber for the king's mummified body. The only entrance was a narrow passage. When the door to the burial chamber had been sealed the passage was filled in and the entrance hidden, in the hope that tomb-robbers would never find it. Yet despite the greatest secrecy, almost all these royal tombs were robbed, probably in times of disorder and lawlessness.

Gizeh was really the cemetery of the Pharaohs of this time. Their pyramids were surrounded by the smaller pyramids of their wives and relatives, and by the flat-topped tombs, called *mastabas*, of the nobles.

A mastaba

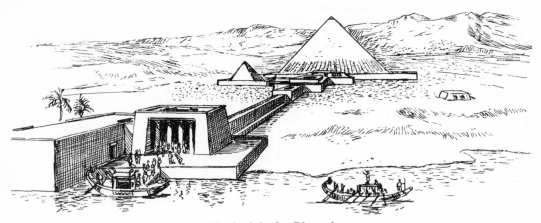

The burial of a Pharaoh

THE BURIAL OF A PHARAOH

The pyramids were built on the desert plateau. Some distance away, a canal was dug so that the royal body could be brought by water to the landing-stage of the Valley Building. Here the body was mummified. That is, it was treated with spices and ointments and wrapped in linen bandages to preserve the flesh. The mummy was dragged on a decorated sledge up a long causeway to the Burial Temple. After a service to the gods, it was finally placed in the pyramid.

Since the Egyptians believed that the dead man returned each day to the chapel, gifts of food and drink were left for him. The chamber to which he would return was most wonderfully decorated and furnished.

The Second Pyramid at Gizeh was built by Pharaoh Khafre and, near it, the Sphinx, a gigantic portrait-head of the king with the body of a crouching lion. Altogether there were more than sixty pyramids on the west side of the Nile.

Later, the Pharaohs gave up building pyramids. Instead, they were buried in tombs hewn out of the rocky hill-sides of a valley far to the south—the Valley of the Kings, near *Thebes*.

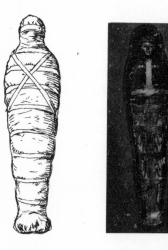

Mummy   *Mummy-case*

THE MIDDLE KINGDOM

The Old Kingdom of the Pyramid Age broke up in a series of rebellions against the Pharaoh. After a time of disorder, new dynasties of wise Pharaohs united the country and there followed the period known as the *Middle Kingdom*.

The great pillars of the temple of Amen-Ra at Karnak, which still stand today

AMEN-RA

The capital of the Middle Kingdom was at *Thebes*, a city which was to surpass all others in magnificence. The special god of Thebes was Ammon or *Amen*, and, as the wealth and power of the city grew, so the importance of Amen increased until he was looked upon as the same as Ra, the Sun-god. Thus, he was known as *Amen-Ra*, greatest of all the gods.

GREATNESS OF THE MIDDLE KINGDOM

Under the Pharaohs of the Middle Kingdom vast temples were built at Thebes, canals were dug, splendid buildings and statues were raised and trade flourished.

A *Suez Canal* was dug from the Red Sea westward to the Delta of the Nile. Through this canal Pharaoh's ships could sail southwards to the mysterious *Land of Punt*, in East Africa, whence they brought back strange and valuable goods. To the north, ships ventured on the sea to trade with the Mediterranean Islands.

In this age Pharaoh began to keep a standing army. The army protected his wealth and added to his Kingdom by conquering Nubia, lying south of the First Cataract.

A model of an early Egyptian ship with its oarsmen

A wall-carving showing an Egyptian attack on the Hittite fortress of Dapur. The Egyptian troops are already placing their scaling ladders. Some of the Hittites are being hauled up into the city by ropes, the gates having been shut upon them.

THE EMPIRE

Suddenly the power of the Pharaohs collapsed and the Middle Kingdom came to an end. A strange enemy called the Shepherd Kings, or *Hyksos*, appeared and conquered Egypt almost without a blow, because they had learned to use chariots and horses.

After about 200 years the Shepherd Kings were driven out. There followed the third and most glorious period of Egypt's history.

Under a series of strong Pharaohs, Egypt extended her power and increased her riches. The army, chiefly composed of archers, spearmen and war-chariots, conquered an empire of many peoples.

This empire stretched, at times, from the River Euphrates in Asia, through Syria and Palestine to Nubia and the Land of Punt in Africa; it was an empire over 2,000 miles long.

The great Pharaohs included *Thotmes I* who reconquered Nubia and went northwards victoriously to the Euphrates. He added to the temple of Amen at *Karnak*, adjoining the city of Thebes, which gradually became the greatest temple ever known.

Ancient Egyptian warriors

A GREAT QUEEN OF EGYPT

Thotmes' successor married a lady named *Hatshepsut*, the first great woman in history.

Queen Hatshepsut was a remarkable woman who took the unheard-of step of ruling her country. Dressed as a man, she retained complete power for twenty years. One of her famous acts was to send an expedition to Punt. Her eight ships sailed down the Red Sea and eventually returned with cargoes of fine woods, myrrh, ebony, ivory, gold, cinnamon, " eye-paint," apes, monkeys, leopard-skins and " incense-trees " to plant in her temple-gardens.

THE REVENGE OF THOTMES III

When the Queen died, her nephew, Thotmes III, ordered her name to be erased from every monument and her statues to be smashed.

The head of Queen Hatshepsut carved in green slate

Thotmes III, though spiteful to his aunt, was a great general who extended Egypt's rule as far as the Greek Islands. He, too, was a zealous builder of temples and obelisks, tall monumental pillars, in many parts of Egypt. His masterpiece was the gigantic colonnade at Karnak.

Queen Hatshepsut's ships arrive in the Land of Punt

Akhn-aten and Nefertiti at dinner in their palace

A NEW RELIGION

Amenhotep IV was a delicate child who became Pharaoh when a young man. He came to believe that the Sun-god was God, not merely of Egypt, but of all the world, and also, that he was the *only* god. He called his god *Aten* and commanded the people to worship Aten and forget all other gods.

He changed his name to Akhn-aten (" Spirit of Aten "), and left Thebes to build a new capital at a place now called *Amarna*. Here he raised a splendid temple to Aten and, with his lovely young wife Nefertiti, almost retired from the business of ruling his empire. Instead, he tried to teach his people to follow his new religion of honesty and goodness, and he wrote exceedingly beautiful poetry to his god.

In vain the governors wrote beseeching him to send troops. One by one, his father's territories were lost; Syria was over-run by the Hittites; Palestine was invaded by the Hebrews. The Empire began to crumble.

Akhn-aten's successor was his son-in-law, *Tut-enkh-aten*, but the priests of the old god soon changed this to Tut-enkh-*amen*. He died when he was only eighteen.

THE TOMB OF TUT-ENKH-AMEN

Tut-enkh-amen was buried in a cliff-tomb surrounded by all the magnificent furniture, ornaments and paintings proper to a Pharaoh.

Tut-enkh-amen and his queen in their palace

CONQUEST OF EGYPT

Eventually, Thebes itself was sacked by the *Assyrians*. Later, in 525 B.C., the Persian king, *Cambyses*, conquered the whole country, and Egypt became a province of the *Persian Empire*, until *Alexander the Great* placed it under Greek rule.

When Alexander died, Egypt fell to one of his generals named *Ptolemy*, who became founder of a new line of kings known as the Ptolemies.

These riches were never plundered because workmen, digging the tomb for a later Pharaoh, threw out an immense quantity of stone chippings which completely covered the entrance to Tut-enkh-amen's tomb.

The tomb was quite forgotten for 3000 years, until, in 1922, a party of archaeologists discovered it and revealed to the world the astounding riches of this ancient land.

Under them, Egypt again became rich and powerful, especially at sea. In 31 B.C. the Roman emperor *Octavian* defeated Mark Antony and Cleopatra, and the rule of the Ptolemies came to an end. Egypt became a province of the great *Roman Empire*.

The great colossus of Rameses II

EGYPT'S DECLINE

The power of the Empire recovered somewhat under the next family of kings known as the Nineteenth Dynasty. *Seti I* and *Rameses II* were warlike Pharaohs, but after their rule Egypt gradually declined, as her enemies grew strong on every side.

Egyptian farmworkers ploughing, sowing, and taking stock of the seed

2. HOW PEOPLE LIVED IN ANCIENT EGYPT

RULERS AND WORKERS

There were two distinct classes of people in Ancient Egypt : those who were educated leaders, and the vast majority who laboured to build and maintain a magnificent civilization.

The king or Pharaoh lived in great splendour, surrounded by his nobles and Court Officials. The priests were a powerful and privileged class, with great wealth as well as tremendous influence over the king and his people.

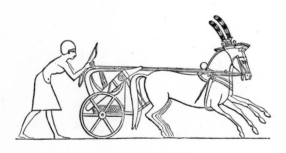

Servant with chariot

The workers included skilled craftsmen such as scribes, goldsmiths and masons ; and labourers in the fields and quarries, who were little better than slaves.

FARMING

Probably the lives of the workers changed little in the 4,000 years of Ancient Egypt's history.

Pictures on the walls of chapels belonging to noblemen show how important was the work of the farm.

We see the labourers sowing and reaping, pouring water into the channels which irrigated the land, and reaping the ripe grain with wooden sickles. We see them tending their cattle and loading donkeys with the harvest, while a scribe jots down details for his lord.

CRAFTSMEN

Pictures in the tombs also tell us much about the craftsmen. The coppersmith could make a saw for wood, as well as another for the great blocks of stone used in pyramids and temples. There were potters making fine vessels to be baked in a closed furnace.

Dish with handle and fish design, probably for holding ointment or face cream

Other craftsmen made tiles covered with brilliant-coloured glaze for the walls of splendid houses. Later, they learned how to make bottles and vases of glass, which were eagerly bought by people of other races.

The Egyptians excelled in making jewellery and ornaments. The goldsmith's work has never been bettered and there were craftsmen called *lapidaries*, skilled in cutting semi-precious stones. Tiny pieces of coloured stone were fitted together to make patterns set in gold.

Weaving seems to have been done chiefly by women, and their work was so fine that it cannot be equalled by modern machines. Since the weather was almost always hot, linen, not wool, was woven on the hand looms. Linen cloth was needed for clothes and also for awnings and hangings in the great houses.

There were, of course, many other workers ; there were cabinet-makers, personal servants, boat-builders and papyrus-gatherers ; soldiers and embalmers of the dead, as well as the humble labourers who made bricks.

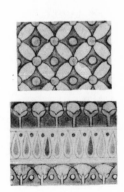

These are some of the designs which the Egyptians wove into their linen

Foreign captives making bricks and building a wall

HOUSES OF ANCIENT EGYPT

HOMES OF THE WORKERS

The houses of ordinary people were made of sun-dried brick. In towns, these houses were built in long rows or terraces, with all the doors facing on to narrow streets. The windows were small and high up in the walls, to give some light but to keep out the heat.

A worker's house

Inside was the living-room and behind that the bedroom. Some houses seem to have had an entrance lobby with the living-room behind and built higher, so that the windows looked on to the roofs of lobby and bedroom. Behind the house was a yard, with an oven in one corner.

The walls were decorated with paintings but there was little furniture ; perhaps a wooden bed, a few cooking-pots, a large water jar and some sacred charms or amulets.

Steps led from the yard to the flat roof where people slept and took their meals in the evening. On top of the terrace houses, a householder fenced off his piece of roof from his neighbour's.

In the yard the housewife did her cooking, using charcoal for the brick oven. Here, too, the donkey was tethered.

A NOBLEMAN'S HOUSE

Near the river, in walled gardens, shady with trees, stood the houses of the great nobles. Each villa, built of brick and wood, was large and airy. It probably had two storeys, the upper one being for women. In Thebes itself, where land was expensive, the well-to-do possessed houses several storeys high.

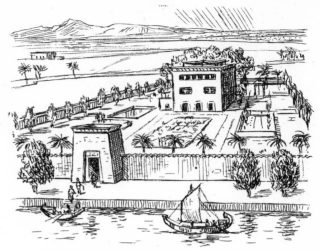

A nobleman's house

The great houses by the river were gaily decorated with painted walls and patterned hangings. Columns supporting the blue starry ceilings were shaped like palm trees or lotus stalks, and the floors were tiled with pictures of fish and river creatures.

A visitor entered the house through a portico leading into a spacious entrance hall. The central room of the house was sometimes an open courtyard with the inner rooms leading from it. There were the lord's private chambers, bedrooms, guest rooms and the women's quarters.

Outside were the servants' rooms, kitchens, stables and, by the time of the Empire, a chariot store. There were yards for cattle and a row of corn bins like huge bee-hives.

Furniture in the house was made of costly wood, such as ebony.

inlaid with ivory. Beds were much like our own, but had a mesh of plaited palm fibre where we should have a spring-base. Instead of pillows, wooden neck-rests, sometimes richly carved, were used.

Egyptian houses had no cupboards. Food was kept in large jars, and linen and other household goods were stored in wooden chests or skilfully woven baskets.

Inside the house of a wealthy family

Music and dancing at a feast

DAILY LIFE

FOOD

Most Egyptians did not eat very much meat, but poor people ate a good deal of fish which they caught from the Nile by means of nets and spears. Geese, ducks and wild fowl were snared in large numbers in the marshes of the Delta. Hunting-parties, in shallow boats, provided themselves with nets, throwing-sticks and even hunting-cats.

Flat, round loaves of wheat or barley were baked at home and beer was drunk by all classes of people.

Fishing

The Egyptians loved feasting and drinking. Many kinds of meat, poultry, bread, cakes, fruit and sweets were served to rich guests, who helped themselves daintily with their fingers from various bowls placed on low tables.

MUSIC

While the feast progressed, music entertained the company. The chief instruments were the stringed guitar, the harp and lyre. With them were played pipes, flute, cymbals and tambourine.

Then came the dancers. They were slaves, since dancing was only watched by the upper classes, who did not take part. The dancing consisted largely of graceful movements of the body and arms. Usually the dancers performed in twos to the music of players who were seated cross-legged on the floor.

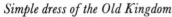

Simple dress of the Old Kingdom   *Tut-enkh-amen wearing the Khat head-dress*   *Queen Nefertiti*

CLOTHES

In the days of the Old Kingdom men wore a simple kilt, and the women wore a long, tight-fitting tunic which left the arms bare. Hair was cut short so that wigs could be worn, except by priests and the poor.

During the time of the Middle Kingdom and the Empire, head-dresses became more and more elaborate.

There was the strange double-crown of Pharaoh showing the uniting of the two kingdoms. Other head-dresses included religious symbols such as the sun's disk, ram's horns, snakes and the Isis hawk. There was also the striped linen head-dress known as the " Khat," which was worn by the effigy of Tut-enkh-amen on his golden coffin.

Wall-paintings and gigantic statues show us that robes were made of almost transparent linen, starched and pleated with elaborate skill.

Jewellery became increasingly costly and beautiful, and usually took the form of necklaces for both men and women, and large pendants known as pectorals. Queen Nefertiti here, wife of Akhn-aten, wears a high cap and necklace and she seems to have followed the fashion of completely shaving the head, since not a vestige of hair can be seen.

People seem to have gone bare-foot until the time of the Empire, when the nobility wore sandals.

Pharaoh and Queen

THE CITY OF THEBES

Queen Hatshepsut's temple at Thebes

Built on both sides of the Nile, Thebes was the capital and religious centre of Egypt for centuries. In the middle stood the royal palace and gardens, surrounded by the houses of the great nobles.

The Avenue of Sphinxes at Thebes

On every side towering obelisks were covered with carvings, and gigantic statues proclaimed the might of the Pharaohs.

The vast temples of *Karnak* and *Luxor* stood north and south of the city. The temple of Amen at Karnak was the greatest building ever erected, and the pillars of its nave were so vast that it is said that 100 men could stand on the top of each. The doors were over-laid with gold and decorated with precious stones and blue lapis lazuli. An avenue of sphinxes, more than a mile long, led to the river.

BUILDING THE TEMPLES

How were these mighty temples raised and how were their roofs and pillars so gorgeously decorated? It is believed that when the first stages of the walls and the bases of the columns had been raised, the whole of the interior was filled with earth. Stones for the next course were dragged up earth ramps into position, and more earth was added inside.

Eventually the roof was reached, and by the time it was completed the whole temple had been filled with earth. This earth was scooped out gradually, so that the painters and artists could decorate from the top down.

Pharaoh approaches the scales in which his good deeds are weighed against his evil deeds

RELIGION

The Egyptians believed in many gods of whom the greatest was Ra, the Sun-god, though the Theban god, Amen, became identified with the Sun-god as Amen-Ra. There was *Osiris*, god of the Nile and of life ; oddly enough, he was also god of the Underworld, or kingdom of the dead. There were gods peculiar to each city and others which took the form of animals, such as *Anubis*, the jackal-headed god, and *Amemit* the Devourer, with crocodile head, fore-parts of a lion and hindquarters of a hippopotamus.

Since the Egyptians believed in a life after death, those who were rich and powerful enough took enormous trouble to make sure that their bodies were preserved forever. That is why the pyramids and the rock tombs were built at such cost.

To help the dead man, certain rolls of papyrus were placed in the tomb. These were covered with writings and pictures giving instructions for the journey, as well as the prayers and hymns which he would need. A roll of this kind was very long, sometimes as much as ninety feet, and was called *The Book of the Dead.*

Furniture and food were left in the tomb or its chapel for the use of the dead man. On the difficult journey through the Underworld he would have to answer questions of forty-two gods with such names as the Eater of Blood, Breaker of Bones and Eye of Flame.

The mummy of Hunefer, a royal scribe, being prepared for its journey to the next world

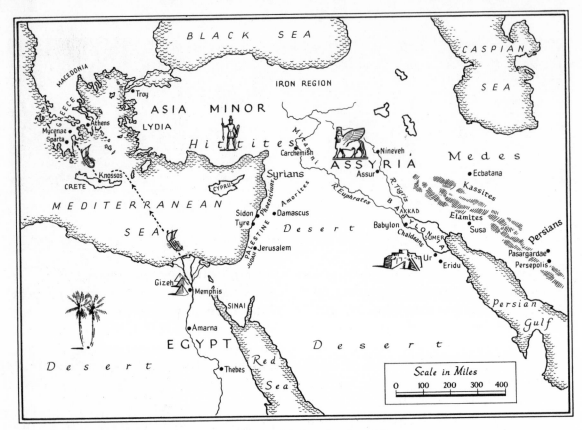

The Ancient world before the rise of Rome

PART TWO : THE LAND OF TWO RIVERS

3. THE SUMERIANS

THE FIRST SETTLERS

Nearly 1,000 miles east of the Nile Delta, two great rivers flow into the Persian Gulf. They are the Euphrates and the Tigris. To the west of their valley lies the Syrian desert, and to the east the Persian mountains. This long, fertile valley has had several names, for it was first known as the Plain of Shinar, then Babylonia, and, much later, Mesopotamia, which means " between the rivers." Its modern name is Iraq.

The climate of the Land of Two Rivers was similar to Egypt's, and the soil, being river silt, gave equally rich harvests when watered from canals and irrigation ditches. Thus a civilization arose here as early as, or even earlier than in Egypt itself. The first people probably came from the mountains to the east and made their huts of plaited reeds daubed with mud. Their land became known as *Sumer*.

24

Sumerian pottery, found at Ur

The early Sumerians were Stone Age farming people. They used copper as a precious metal for ornaments, but they had no bronze. Their knives, hoes and axes were made of flint and hard rock-crystal from the desert, since their land had no rock of any kind.

These Sumerians wove cloth and possessed beads made of shell and pink pebble, but their greatest skill was in pottery, though they had not learned to use a potter's wheel. The vessels were white or greenish in colour with attractive designs painted in black and brown lines.

THE FLOOD

Suddenly disaster came to this flourishing community. The river waters rose higher than they had ever done before, and the Flood, of which we read in the Bible, drowned most of the people in the valley. When the waters subsided, they left a layer of mud eight to eleven feet thick, and on this mud the survivors, with another wave of settlers, began to build a new civilization.

The settlers came from the north, bringing metal and the potter's wheel. Having no stone, they built their houses and temples with bricks made from the river mud, and dried in the sun, or better, baked in a kiln.

To ornament the walls of the temples, they pressed little pegs about the size of a crayon painted at one end, into the wet mud plaster. In this way, only the flat painted ends showed in elaborate, highly coloured patterns.

Sumerian brick-built huts

This is one side of a wooden box, known as the standard of Ur. It is covered with mosaic pictures of red and white shell set in blue lapis lazuli. This side shows, at the top, a royal feast. The king and his nobles are drinking, while a musician plays upon a stringed instrument carved in the shape of the sacred bull. Perhaps the king is celebrating a great victory, for the lower two lines of mosaic show servants and soldiers bringing in animals and captured booty. It is thought that the Sumerians carried this standard when they marched in processions.

SUMERIAN CITY-KINGDOMS

By 3000 B.C. a number of city-kingdoms had grown up in Sumeria. *Eridu* was reckoned to be the oldest, *Ur* (the town from which Abraham later set forth) was the greatest, and among others were *Lagash*, *Larsa*, *Kish* and *Erech*. Each city had its leader who ruled over his mud-brick town and the surrounding land, not only as king but also as priest and earthly representative of the local god.

SUMER AND AKKAD

In the same valley, but farther north, was the town of *Akkad*. The country round about had been settled by a warlike nomadic people called *Semites* who had great skill as archers. From them arose the first great Semitic ruler, *King Sargon of Akkad*.

About 2500 B.C. Sargon defeated the city-kingdoms of Sumeria and made himself lord of all the Plain of Shinar. He was careful, though, not to offend the city gods, and sent his own daughter to be High Priestess to the Moon-God of Ur.

After a couple of centuries Sargon's dynasty declined and the city-kingdoms again rose to power, with Ur taking the leadership. But, by now, the Semites and Sumerians were one people, and *King Ur-Nammu*, founder of the Third Dynasty at Ur, was lord of a great and prosperous empire.

UR-NAMMU'S ZIGGURAT

Inside the walled Sacred Area (or *Timenos*) of the city, towered the *Ziggurat*, the temple and dwelling-place of Nannar the Moon-God. It was a vast pile, built in steps like a pyramid.

The centre was solid, being the remains of earlier Ziggurats, and the lowest storey, faced with an eight-feet thick layer of brick, measured over 200 feet in length by 150 feet in width. The walls, sloping slightly inwards, rose sheer for fifty feet and here was built the second storey, a little smaller so that it left a wide terrace all round. Above was the third storey and, on top, the Holy of Holies, the little shrine of Nannar. The temple of his wife, Nin-gal, the Moon-Goddess, was on a lower terrace.

On one side of this mighty pile was a magnificent three-fold stairway. Each part had 100 steps and each converged on a massive gateway from which a single flight led to the top terraces and the shrine.

Although only the high priests could approach the shrine itself, the temple and its Sacred Area, with its store-rooms, courts, priests' dwellings, royal palace, and lesser temples for the ordinary people, gave meaning and purpose to the life of the city.

Ur-Nammu's Ziggurat

A narrow street in Ur

HOUSES

The streets of the city were unpaved and very narrow, so that two- and four-wheeled carts, pulled by mules, were not permitted to enter the gates. The houses fronting these narrow streets had no lower windows, and the small upper windows had reed

Inside a simple house in Ur

lattices to keep out the glare of the sun. The front door, whose lower hinge-peg turned in a slab of imported stone, led into a small lobby, where a visitor would find a jar of water so that he might wash his feet over a drain in the corner.

The main rooms of a house were built round a central court, which was open to the sky. On the lower floor was the guest room, furnished with rugs to sit on. There were slaves' quarters, storerooms, a lavatory and the kitchen, with its fireplaces, querns and pounders for corn, as well as various pots of clay and copper.

For lavatory and drain each house had a deep pit or soak-away, lined with upright pipes pierced with tiny holes. It was customary when the drain was dug to throw down offerings to please the spirits that dwelt below the earth.

In two-storey houses the family lived upstairs in rooms which led off a wooden verandah built against the walls of the courtyard. Unlike the Egyptians, the Sumerians did not decorate their houses with gay wall-paintings, since it was believed that only white-washed plaster would bring good luck.

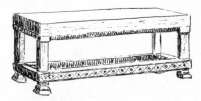

Sumerian furniture

FURNISHINGS

Stools, low chairs and tables furnished the rooms, with cushions and rugs on the floor. Wooden chests and wicker baskets stored clothes and valuable possessions, which included bowls and trinket boxes most skilfully wrought in gold and silver with inlays of shell and precious stones. Cups, bowls and vases were also made of very hard stone such as limestone, diorite, steatite and alabaster brought from the far-off mountains.

CLOTHES

In early times the traditional garment of Sumerians was a sheepskin skirt or kilt, belted or fastened over one shoulder. Usually the wool was left on the sheepskin, and combed or trimmed to give a flounced effect. In cool weather cloaks of leather and felted cloth were worn.

By Ur-Nammu's time long, spade-shaped, curled beards were fashionable, so, too, was a dignified woollen garment like the Roman toga. Ladies wore long, flounced dresses with a draped shawl, and wigs seem to have been worn by noble persons.

The royalty and their court must have been gorgeously dressed. Queen Shub-ad, the wife of one of the early Sumerian rulers, wore this elaborate head-dress over her great wig : it is made of looped gold ribbon, with gold leaves, inlaid with precious stones and fastened with a great comb. Her dress was covered in beads of gold, silver, lapis-lazuli, red carnelian and agate, while her ladies dressed themselves in gay robes of red and silver similarly ornamented.

Queen Shub-ad

The ceremony at the burial of a Sumerian king

RELIGION

The Sumerians believed in a life after death, though apart from one period their burial rites were less complicated than those of the Egyptians. They usually buried their dead in brick or mat-lined shafts dug down under their houses ; this preserved the unity of the family.

A ROYAL BURIAL

Early in the story of Ur, a brick tomb was built at the bottom of a deep pit, one side of which was sloped. The king's body was placed in this tomb, accompanied by his gold-hafted weapons and magnificent gold helmet. Bowls of food and drink, and personal possessions, such as his gold dagger and pencil, were laid at his side. His servants drank from a drugged cup and lay down by their master, whereupon the tomb was bricked up and plastered.

Next occurred an astonishing ceremony. Down the pit slope came a procession of gorgeously dressed people of the Court accompanied by musicians playing on harps and lyres. They were followed by two or more chariots drawn by oxen, carefully manoeuvred down the slope.

Last came a company of soldiers drawn up in ranks. To the sound of music, each drank from his own cup of poisoned or drugged liquid and lay down devoutly for his last sleep. Attendants then slaughtered the animals and the great pit was filled in. Thus the king travelled to the next world, with his possessions, his vehicles and his servants.

Impressions from roller-seals

RICH GODS

The god of a Sumerian city owned land outside the walls, and his estates were worked for him by slaves and labourers, or were rented to farmers.

The produce and rents were brought to the Timenos to be paid to the priests. Since money was not yet used, rents were paid in corn, dates, wool, milk, cheese, butter and farm animals. The priests carefully recorded all these goods and stored them in special rooms round the temple courtyard. Much of the produce went to feed and clothe the numerous priests and priestesses, but there was enough over to send to other lands in exchange for things the god needed, such as building stone, gems, gold, silver and sweet incense.

WRITING

Trade led to the invention, first, of picture-writing, and later of marks or symbols. The Sumerians had no papyrus, but there was plenty of clay, so the scribe used a tablet of soft river mud. It was difficult to scratch marks on this damp surface,

so he pressed into the clay with his pen or stylus, made of bone or hard reed. The end of his pen was cut in the shape of a thin wedge, so he made a series of wedge-shaped marks which were originally picture-shapes, but later became signs for the syllables of words. This wedge-shaped writing is called *cuneiform,* because the Latin word for a wedge is " cuneus." When the clay tablet or cone was baked, it remained hard and almost impossible to destroy. Thousands of these ancient tablets have been dug up and the writing on them can now be understood by experts.

A tablet with cuneiform writing

Traders carrying their goods from the warehouses along the river

TRADE

As you would expect in this long valley, the two great rivers were highways for trade, and from earliest times the Sumerians were boat-builders. They wove reeds and willows because there was no good timber, and covered the stout wicker-work with skins and pitch. Towns were built on the river banks, or were connected to them by broad canals.

Along the quays stood warehouses crammed with goods from the Timenos and from the storerooms of wealthy merchants. The goods were tied up in bales or jars, and when the owner had secured them with rope or a piece of cloth over the mouth of the jar, clay was spread over and the owner's seal pressed or rolled into it while it was wet. The seals bore patterns and figures which were the recognised marks of the owner.

Traders took the goods by boat as far as possible, and then crossed the deserts and mountains with strings of donkeys and camels.

Timber had to be fetched from the forests of far-away Lebanon, silver and copper came from the mines of Asia Minor and Sinai. Precious stones were bargained for in the market at Susa in the mountainous land of the *Elamites*, while spices and incense were brought by sea from India and the Land of Punt. Sea voyages were made in wooden ships which sailed out of the Persian Gulf and hugged the coast until they came to the Red Sea to trade with Egypt.

A caravan of traders sets off across the desert

Hammurabi dictates a message to a scribe

4. BABYLON AND HAMMURABI

The kingdom of Sumer and Akkad was crushed by the Elamites who destroyed the splendours of Ur and of the neighbouring merchant towns, while another Semitic tribe called *Amorites* overran Akkad and seized a little town on the bank of the Euphrates called *Babylon*.

From these Amorite tribesmen emerged *Hammurabi*, the second great Semitic king in history, as Sargon of Akkad was the first. About the year 2000 B.C. he drove out the Elamites and secured the whole of the plain. He then devoted the rest of his life to ruling his kingdom with remarkable vigour and justice.

From his palace at Babylon Hammurabi sent out countless messages,

orders and rebukes to the governors of his cities and provinces. Perhaps a canal required cleaning out, a town wall needed strengthening, taxes must be collected with greater severity, or a religious feast was to be celebrated. The royal scribe wrote down the message with his wedge-ended stylus on a tablet of clay.

Then he sprinkled it with dry powder to prevent it sticking to the clay envelope, which he folded over and handed to a slave to take to an oven to be baked. Shortly afterwards, it was carried by royal messenger to the governor concerned. Nearly 4000 years later, that same message, and many others like it, has been dug up from the mounds of dust and rubble that were once prosperous cities.

HAMMURABI'S CODE OF LAWS

Hammurabi realized that good government depended upon justice which the people could understand, so he collected together the old laws and customs, improved them and added new ones of his own. Then he ordered this Code of Laws to be engraved on a large stone and set up in the temple of *Marduk*, god of Babylon. Copies of Hammurabi's Laws were set up in every city of the land.

These famous laws give us a picture of life in those far-off times. Women were treated with honour and were allowed to own property, which was unusual in ancient times ; slaves, of course, belonged to rich men, but they, too, had some rights and were not to be treated cruelly.

All freeborn children were to go to school to learn tablet-writing ; careless workmen were punished and merchants must not charge too much for their goods. Doctors could charge ten shekels of silver for curing the wound of a rich man, but only five shekels if the patient was poor.

This carved stone is called a stele. It is inscribed with Hammurabi's Laws, and at the top there is a carving of Hammurabi himself receiving the laws from the Sun God, who is seated on a throne.

Boys at school in Babylon

Stealing from the palace or the temple courtyards was punished by death, and many of the laws were based on the rule : " An eye for an eye, a tooth for a tooth." One law states that, " if a man has made the tooth of another fall out, one of his own teeth shall be knocked out."

THE FALL OF BABYLON

After Hammurabi's death barbaric mountain tribes overran the rich valley. Babylon was captured and plundered. For the next 1000 years the Land of Two Rivers played little part in the advance of civilization.

5. THE ASSYRIAN EMPIRE

Lying between Egypt and Babylonia, but somewhat to the north, was the land of the *Hittites*, an energetic mountain folk who were the first to make extensive use of iron. Their iron swords and spears were so superior to bronze that the Hittites fought and defeated the armies of Egypt at the time when Akhnaten was devoting himself to his new religion.

The northernmost part of the valley of the River Tigris was known as *Assur*, and this was also the name of the local god.

The people of Assur, known as *Assyrians*, were fighters and traders, who had learned the arts of commerce and of cuneiform writing from the Babylonians. They had also learned how to tame and use horses from a horse-breeding tribe called the Mitanni, and they had obtained

A colossal human-headed winged lion, which stood in the royal palace at Nimrod

Two warriors of the ninth century B.C. The toothed object held by the warrior at the back is a shield, seen sideways. The other warrior carries a bow and arrow

iron from the Hittites. Tough and quick to learn from their neighbours, the Assyrians possessed their own brand of ferocity in war.

In an age of cruelty the Assyrians outdid their rivals in cruelty. From about 850 B.C., they swept across the Middle East like a torrent, finding no one to stand for long against their fighting methods and their savagery.

Assur-bani-pal's archers make an advance in chariots against an enemy army

Most of their soldiers were archers, protected by spearmen carrying shields, and supported by ferocious squadrons of horse-drawn chariots.

The massive fortifications of enemy cities did not halt their progress, for the Assyrians were the first to use siege-towers and battering-rams, which made short work of the mud-brick walls. All the riches of the wrecked cities, silver, gold, sheep, cattle, spices, foodstuffs and slaves, were carried away to the Assyrian capital, *Nineveh*, or to its great neighbour *Nimrod*.

ASSYRIAN CONQUESTS

First, Babylon was captured from the Kassites, and then the Assyrians pushed westwards towards the Mediterranean. *Tiglath*, an Assyrian king of the eighth century B.C., invaded Palestine and captured Jerusalem and the great trading city of Damascus. Next the Assyrians turned southwards to overwhelm the cities along the Mediterranean coast which were held by a clever merchant people called the *Phoenicians*. Finally, Egypt itself was subdued.

Assur-bani-pal, 668–626 B.C., most powerful of the Assyrian kings, ruled the greatest empire that the world had yet known.

Assur-bani-pal kills a lion

Inside the royal palace at Nineveh

ASSYRIAN BUILDINGS

The Assyrians had a plentiful supply of building stone in their hills. At Nineveh, therefore, *Sennacherib*, grandfather of Assur-bani-pal, was able to build a magnificent city of both stone and brick, using stone principally for foundations and for ornament. He built the world's first large aqueduct, which brought ample water to the new capital. Then, along the banks of the Tigris, splendid buildings and tower-temples, similar to the ziggurats, were raised inside the walled city.

The palaces were faced with glazed tiles of gorgeous colours, and on either side of the arched gateways stood gigantic carved figures of winged bulls with human heads. The courtyards and temples, vaster than those of Ur and Babylon, were adorned with huge carved friezes, stretching along the walls for hundreds of yards. These stone carvings, some of which can be seen in the British Museum, show wonderful skill and understanding of animals, especially in hunting scenes.

King Assur-bani-pal goes lion-hunting from a chariot. A companion holds the reins while the king takes aim with his bow. Behind the royal chariot come attendants, armed with daggers and shields, to protect the king from the attack of a wounded lion.

A book from Assur-bani-pal's library

The Assyrian kings were the most powerful in the world. Nearly all of them were feared and hated by their subjects. Assur-bani-pal, however, last of the great Assyrian kings, was a scholar who collected over 20,000 clay tablets into the finest library of the time. Here was all the knowledge of the Ancient World set down by the royal scribes in Babylonian wedge-shaped writing. At their master's command, they wrote down some of the hymns and prayers to the old gods, as well as those to their own gods, Assur, and Nebo, god of learning. There were age-old legends and stories too, for it is in Assur-bani-pal's library that we find the legends of the creation of the world and the Flood. Other tablets told about the stars and planets, about medicines, plants, science, mathematics, and there were even dictionaries.

6. THE CHALDEANS: BABYLON AGAIN

THE DEFEAT OF THE ASSYRIANS

A Persian archer

The Assyrian Empire suddenly collapsed before the assaults of two nomadic tribes who for centuries had been thrusting in from the east. The *Chaldeans* first captured Babylon (616 B.C.) which Assur-bani-pal had rebuilt, and then joined the *Medes* in an attack upon Nineveh itself. The proud city was burnt to the ground, and, like the Assyrian empire, never rose again.

The Chaldeans now enjoyed a brief but glorious period. They rebuilt Babylon and made it the capital from which *Nebuchadnezzar* (604–561 B.C.) reigned in such legendary splendour.

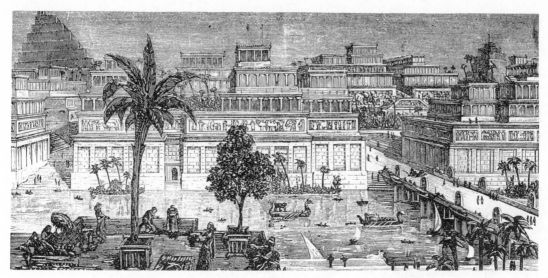

The new Babylon, built by Nebuchadnezzar, must have looked like this

THE REIGN OF NEBUCHADNEZZAR

Nebuchadnezzar ruled for forty years and is chiefly remembered for his rebuilding of Babylon, so that this period is often called the New Babylonian Empire.

NEW BABYLON

The city, said to have been fifteen miles square, was rebuilt on either side of the Euphrates, along whose banks stood thriving warehouses and quays crowded with shipping. A massive wall protected the city, so wide that the top formed a roadway, with covered sidewalks and space for a chariot to drive. Set in this wall were 100 bronze-covered gates, including the huge Ishtar Gate, dedicated to *Ishtar*, goddess of love. A magnificent avenue, called Procession Street, led across the city to the temple area. Here, towering over all, was the Temple of *Marduk*, so lofty

that it seemed to the captive Hebrews to reach almost to the sky.

The blue-tiled gate, built to honour Ishtar

The hanging gardens of Babylon

These gardens were so carefully watered from a specially dug canal that they seemed to hang down in rich profusion, and were called the Hanging Gardens of Babylon. They were built to please the queen, and were known to the Greeks as one of the Seven Wonders of the World.

Near the Ishtar Gate, Nebuchadnezzar built his fabulous palace, decorated, not with stone friezes, since stone was scarcer than in Assur, but with brilliantly coloured tiles, arranged in patterns and pictures. Nebuchadnezzar had gardens laid out in terraces around the palace, one above another, and planted with trees, shrubs and flowers.

ASTROLOGY

The old gods were still worshipped, with Marduk and Ishtar now occupying the places of honour. There was much interest in foretelling the future and in the positions of the stars. A priest, called a diviner, would examine the liver of a sacrificed sheep in order to predict the future.

A priest examines a sheep's liver

Other men, especially the Chaldeans, developed a great deal of knowledge of the movements of the planets, which were believed to affect the lives of men on earth. This ancient practice is called *astrology* and it has had its followers for centuries down to the present day. Though it included a great deal of superstition, there was also genuine observation of the heavens, and this was the beginning of the science of astronomy.

A squadron of mounted Persian archers

7. THE PERSIANS

THE CONQUESTS OF CYRUS

The Chaldean Empire lasted only seventy-three years and the glories of Nebuchadnezzar did not last long after his death.

Centuries earlier (about 1600 B.C.), nomadic tribes moved from the vast steppe-lands of northern Europe and Asia, seeking pasture for their flocks. They were not Semites, but a race called *Aryans.* One large group settled in India, and others made their way into the mountainous country we call Persia, where they occupied much of the land of the Elamites.

These *Persians,* as vassals, had joined forces with their kinsmen, the *Medes,* to defeat Assyria. Suddenly, in about 550 B.C., the Persians overthrew the Medes through the dazzling genius of their leader *Cyrus,* "the Great King."

But before the fall of Babylon, the energy of Cyrus and the deadly skill of his Persian soldiers had already astounded the world. His army was largely composed of archers who let fly a deadly hail of arrows before the foe could come to grips with them, whereupon the cavalry, from both wings, swept down to complete the victory.

A great alliance was formed against the Persians, consisting of Egypt and the city-states of Asia Minor, but Cyrus struck so swiftly that the whole of Asia Minor was crushed.

Cyrus was killed in battle, but four years later his son *Cambyses* conquered Egypt itself (525 B.C.) and the rule of the Persians stretched from the Nile Delta across the whole civilized world to the borders of India.

Darius the Great (521-485), who succeeded the half-mad Cambyses, was not only a soldier but a wise ruler of his vast domains. He pushed eastward to India and north into Russia, where he found the climate too cold for his soldiers. So he turned westwards to tackle the rising power of the *Greeks*, but, as we shall learn later, his army of 50,000 men was defeated on the plain of *Marathon*.

After Darius died, his son *Xerxes* carried on the war against Greece, but again his army was soundly, if surprisingly, beaten.

A number of weak and often cruel rulers followed Xerxes, until the last of the line, Darius III, was defeated by *Alexander the Great* and Persia became part of the Macedonian Empire.

King Darius I

THE PERSIAN CIVILIZATION

Since the Persians had advanced in half a century from peasant-farmers to world conquerors, they had much to learn from their new subjects.

WRITING

All business and trade gradually came to be conducted in *Aramaic,* the language of Syrian merchants, which had steadily made its way throughout the Middle East. The old Babylonian and Assyrian languages and their wedge-shaped writing slowly died out. The Persians used a cuneiform alphabet of thirty-nine letters which had certain connections with the older Babylonian writing, but they preferred to use ink and parchment as writing materials.

Conquered princes submitting to King Darius

GOVERNMENT

Darius divided his empire into twenty provinces, each ruled by a *satrap*, or governor, whose duties were to check revolt and to raise taxes from the landowners and farmers. Darius treated his peoples with a kindliness that was remarkable in days when a defeated foe could expect the most ruthless cruelty.

RESPECT FOR LEARNING

Darius was anxious to learn new facts about the world he had won. He encouraged the Chaldean astrologers at Babylon to pursue their knowledge, and he founded a medical school at Sais, in Egypt.

More surprising still, since the Persians were an inland people, Darius wished to extend his power and knowledge of the sea. So he sent one of his captains, named Scylax, to explore the River Indus and then to sail along the coast from India into the Red Sea. Stone tablets have been found which show that Darius restored the ancient but disused canal which connected the Nile to the Red Sea at the Gulf of Suez. " Then this canal was dug as I commanded, and ships sailed from Egypt through this canal to Persia according to my will."

ARCHITECTURE

The Persians built huge temples and palaces with wide terraces, noble staircases and tall columns of cedar

An archer of King Darius' bodyguard

wood, but, as might be expected, they borrowed much from the Babylonian style of building. Their carvings and huge winged bulls were imitated from the Assyrians, while the glazed tiles and flat lintel-stones came from Egypt.

The gateway at Persepolis

The god Mithras killing a bull

RELIGION

Contrary to Greek and Roman stories, the Persians were far from being habitually cruel and barbarous. Darius, especially, felt it his duty to

A winged sphinx from the palace at Nineveh

rule justly, and one of his inscriptions says, " I was not wicked, nor was I a liar, nor was I a tyrant. I have ruled according to righteousness."

This respect for good conduct was the product of the Persian religion, the noblest set of beliefs until Christianity arose. Its founder was a Median prophet named *Zoroaster*, who taught that life was a struggle between Good and Evil. Good was called *Mazda*, " Lord of Wisdom," and his chief helper was *Mithras* " the Light." The spirit of Evil was called *Ahriman*, a figure like Satan of the Hebrews. Zoroaster taught that every man must choose between Good and Evil, and that he would be judged in afterlife. This belief in judgment and in afterlife raised the standard of men's lives in Ancient Egypt, in Persia and later in Christian communities.

The Persian religion spread far and wide, not only because it gave hope to even the lowliest of mortals, but because of the attraction of the spirit Mithras. He came to be thought of as the Sun-God, and was especially popular with Roman soldiers, so that temples for his worship have been found as far away as in Britain.

PEOPLE AND EVENTS TO REMEMBER

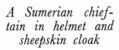

In this book there has not been space to deal separately with the history of the Hebrews, but to help you to place some of the events of the Old Testament, one or two dates, marked by an asterisk, are given below.

(Dates before about 1500 B.C. are uncertain, and you will find that even the experts disagree about them.)

A Sumerian chieftain in helmet and sheepskin cloak

A Sumerian in sheepskin kilt carrying a mason's basket

Perhaps 4000 B.C.	Civilization arising in Sumeria	about 1000	Decline of Egypt
			*Kingdom of Saul and David
3300	Menes, Pharaoh of the First Dynasty	850–626	The Assyrian Empire
3000–2600	Pyramids built at Gizeh	732	Assyrians captured Damascus
	City Kingdoms in Sumeria	700	Sennacherib
2500	Sargon of Akkad	668–626	Assur-bani-pal at Nineveh
2250	Ur-Nammu's ziggurat	612	Medes destroy Nineveh
2100–1750	Middle Kingdom of Egypt	604–561	Nebuchadnezzar, King of Babylon
2000	Hammurabi, King of Babylon		*Babylonian captivity of the Hebrews
1750–1550	Shepherd Kings (Hyksos) in Egypt	539	Cyrus of Persia captured Babylon
1550–1205	Empire of Egypt	525	Persians conquered Egypt
	Rise of the Hittites		
about 1370	Akhn-aten and Queen Nefertiti	521–485	Darius the Great
,, 1200	*Moses led the Israelites out of Egypt	333	Persia overthrown by Alexander

Milking cows and making butter in Ur. On the right two farmworkers are milking cows. The milk is then taken through the gateway to the dairy. There it is churned in the great earthenware jar which the dairyworker is rolling from side to side. Two other workers are straining the butter, and the man on the far left is putting away a jar in which the butter is to be stored.

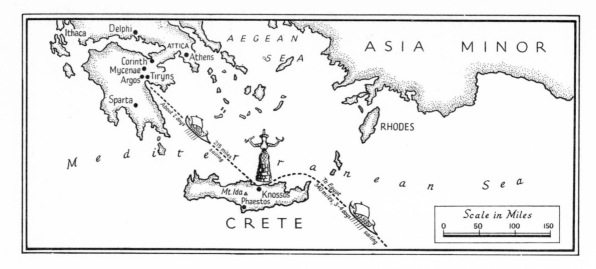

Crete and Greece

PART THREE: ANCIENT GREECE

8. CRETE

Quite recently, it was discovered that there was once, among the islands of the Aegean Sea and on the mainland of Greece, a civilization far older than anyone had suspected. It flourished about 2000 B.C.

Crete was the centre of this civilization, called *Minoan*, because its kings may all have been called Minos. The capital of Crete was Knossos, where Minos built a splendid palace whose innumerable rooms and corridors gave rise to the story of the labyrinth. Doubtless the mainland people paid tribute to Minos, and it is possible that captives were thrown into the bull-ring.

Female athletes in the bull-ring

46

A Minoan harvest procession

The Minoans or Cretans seem to have loved the excitement of bull-fighting and of a marvellous form of entertainment with wild bulls. Wall-paintings show acrobats performing extraordinary feats of skill, vaulting from the charging bull's horn on to its back, and somersaulting to the ground.

LIFE IN CRETE

The Minoans were a talented and artistic people who traded throughout the Eastern Mediterranean and especially with Egypt. Their island had plenty of timber and stone, and its climate was ideal for growing crops of every kind, but the narrow valleys could not produce sufficient corn. So the Minoans took to the sea to become traders.

Their ships carried cargoes not only for themselves but for other peoples less ready to venture on the sea. In order to buy metals, luxuries and corn, the Cretans sold wine, oil, purple cloth, finely wrought jewellery, knives and pottery.

The skill of the Minoan craftsmen is best seen in the wonderful painted pottery which was exported to countries round the eastern end of the Mediterranean.

The pots, bowls and vases were exquisitely shaped and often no thicker than an egg-shell. They were decorated with patterns in colour on a black ground.

The throne in the palace at Knossos

and easy on this lovely island that, in later days, the inhabitants did not build walls or fortifications.

At Knossos the palace of King Minos stood on a little hill ; the centre of the palace was a grand courtyard surrounded by buildings several storeys high.

There were royal apartments, store-rooms, and a maze of passages and small rooms for the king's craftsmen. There was also a theatre or arena where the entertainments took place.

KNOSSOS

Trade made Crete wealthy, so that her sea-kings were able to build fine towns, usually a short distance from the sea but connected with a harbour by a paved road. Life seemed so safe

The walls of the palace rooms were gaily painted with pictures of birds, plants and sea-creatures. Everywhere was the sign of the double-axe, the symbol of Crete's Mother-goddess.

A room in the palace at Knossos

A border for a skirt or kilt using the sign of the double-axe as a repeating pattern

A Cretan flower design, also used on fabric

HOUSES

Since the valleys were used for corn-growing, towns were built on the sides of the hills, so that the main street rose like a long flight of steps, and rooms in the houses were often at different levels.

A narrow street in Crete

The houses were built of timber and brick, with windows quite like our own, though oiled parchment took the place of glass panes. There were staircases inside, and bathrooms and lavatories supplied with water from springs. Skin rugs covered the floors and benches.

Embroidered hangings curtained the doors, and the elegant furniture was made by craftsmen.

FALL OF CRETE

We do not know a great deal about the government and religion of these remarkable people because, although they wrote a form of early Greek, it has not yet yielded much information. We know that disaster overwhelmed them and wiped out the splendours of Knossos, so that the Minoans were forgotten for centuries. Several earthquakes had caused the city to be rebuilt more than once, and then invaders from the mainland of Greece sacked the unprotected town.

A group of Minoans: a woman bearing an offering, a priestess with snakes, and a cup-bearer

L.A.H.—D

9. THE GREEKS

EARLY WARRIORS

Mycenean huntress

A young prince of Boeotia

On the mainland, at this time, lived people who were probably kinsfolk of the Minoans. They lived in small towns protected by remarkable fortifications, and were prosperous, though not perhaps as advanced as their Minoan cousins. Mycenae was the most powerful town, with Sparta, Argos, Tiryns and Corinth already well known.

Mycenean warrior with plumed helmet

These citadels were attacked by invaders from the North called *Achaeans*. They were tall, brown-haired people armed with iron-tipped weapons, which enabled them to capture Mycenae and the other fortress towns. Some took to the sea, and pushing on from island to island, reached Crete, where they may have finally destroyed a civilization that was already in decay.

Mycenean warrior with leather helmet

The Lion Gate at Mycenae

The Achaeans were followed by an even fiercer people called *Dorians*, who drove them out and overran the southern part of Greece, capturing Sparta, Corinth and Argos. In *Sparta*, particularly, the Dorians lived as warlike conquerors, making the defeated people labour as slaves. The *Ionians*, an adventurous and energetic people, seized Attica, where *Athens* became their chief city, just as Sparta was the leading city of the Dorians.

An early Greek dagger, ornamented with a design showing Greek warriors

A Greek warship

THE FIRST GREEK CIVILIZATION

Gradually these invaders settled down into a way of life that developed into the Greek civilization. In their poems and songs they looked back to these stormy times as an age of great deeds and heroes.

The poet Homer tells us about the early days of the race in two great poems, the *Iliad* and the *Odyssey*, which describe the Siege of Troy, and the adventures of Odysseus.

THE CITY-STATES

The Greeks called themselves *Hellenes*. They felt that they were one race, speaking the same language and worshipping the same gods. But the small communities, often cut off from each other by mountain and sea, came to love their cities more than their country. They were constantly quarrelling and were seldom able to unite, even against a common enemy.

The centre of each city was usually a fortress set on a hill, or *acropolis*. This served as the palace of the king and as a refuge in war. Below the fortress were the simple houses of the citizens and, outside the walls, the farms of the landowners.

A heavy-armed foot soldier

Greek warriors fighting : a messenger is separating them

An early Greek chariot, drawn by four horses

THE " HEROES "

At first the Greeks resembled the Vikings of later days. Following a warrior-king, they devoted themselves to plundering by sea and land, leaving the farmwork to servants.

Their armour and some of their weapons were bronze, but iron was the superior metal for the fighting-man. They carried spears, round shields, swords and a curious " bent-back " bow made of wood covered with ibex-horn. Great skill was required to bend and string it.

Chariots were made of wicker and were used in war and for peaceful travelling. From the body of the car protruded a long pole to which two horses were yoked. Later, four horses were used, two probably attached by long traces.

Ships were undecked galleys, propelled by a single sail, with an oar for rudder. The mast was a straight pine set in a cross-plank, with stays, or ropes, of ox-hide. The sail was rarely lowered but was furled by brailing (that is, by rolling it up in a series of tucks). Since a single sail was useless when the wind was contrary, there were twenty or forty oarsmen. Later, when the Greeks gave up plundering and took to peaceful trading, the merchant ship used a sail only. The warships were oared galleys. The Corinthians became the foremost maritime traders in the early days.

Greek merchant ship

Preparing the wool for spinning

Using a distaff and spindle

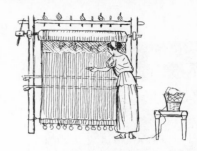
Weaving at a loom

EVERYDAY LIFE IN HOMERIC GREECE

Although the poet loves to stress the riches and splendour which surrounded his heroes, it is clear that life was still crude in some respects. The house or " palace " of the king was timber-framed and brick-built, and its inner walls were plastered and painted. In the courtyard of the palace stood an altar for the sacrifice of animals before a feast.

Various rooms, such as the women's quarters, upper rooms and a bath-house, were built near the men's Hall. This resembled the home of a Saxon chief. There was a porch, vestibule and the hall itself, with its central fireplace, a gallery and a raised seat for the king. On the walls hung shields and spears, but the furniture was finer than anything found in Saxon times.

As well as chests and benches covered with skins, there were three-legged chairs and tables inlaid with silver and gold. There were beautifully made pots, and drinking vessels of silver.

CLOTHES

Women, as always in Greece, had little share in the management of affairs ; their duty was to grind the corn, to cook, serve the food and, of course, to make the clothes. The unmarried women and girls combed and dyed the fleece, twisted the carded wool and spun it into yarn.

Then the weaving women stood at the loom and wove fine cloth of lovely colours—sea-purple, blue and deep violet were highly thought of.

Maidservants prepare a Greek bride for her wedding

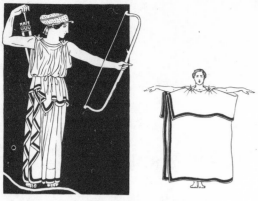

The Dorian chiton

The Ionian chiton with a himation over it

Men wore short tunics at work and in battle, with thicker cloaks fastened by handsome brooches. On more dignified occasions, a long loose robe was worn, which often left the right shoulder bare.

Women wore a loose dress (the *chiton*) in either the Dorian or the Ionian style. The Dorian dress was simply a large piece of cloth, about as wide as both outstretched arms, folded over at the top, and fastened

Men's dress: Zeus and Hermes wearing the fashionable dress

on each shoulder by a brooch. It was gathered at the waist by a girdle.

The Ionian chiton had no fold at the top, but was pinned or sewn along the arms. These dresses were made of fine linen or muslin, sometimes coloured or striped. On cool evenings, and out of doors, a shawl (*himation*) or cloak was worn.

Greek clothing, even in the greatest days, changed little from these simple styles, except that dyed and embroidered patterns became more common. Women's dresses at a later period were made of fine, almost transparent linen, so that the women needed cloaks or shawls outdoors.

GREEK RELIGION

The Greeks had many gods who were wilful and hard to please. A man had always to be careful not to offend them, even in quite small matters, such as pruning vines or crossing a stream.

Zeus was the supreme god, ruling his difficult family at their home on Mount Olympus. His wife was Hera, and their children included Athena, goddess of wisdom, Apollo, god of light, who became more beloved than Zeus himself, Artemis the huntress and Hermes the swift-footed messenger. Poseidon, god of the sea, was brother to Zeus and he sometimes defied him.

There were also Ares, god of war ; Aphrodite, goddess of love ; Dionysus, the wine god, and Hephaestos, the blacksmith, maker of armour.

The Greeks not only brought offerings to the gods in their temples, but worshipped them at home. The head of the household offered daily prayers and gifts of wine and oil at the family altar. Hestia, goddess of the hearth, was the guardian of the home.

THE ORACLE AT DELPHI

Athens was thought of as the city particularly under the protection of the wise and lovely Athena, but *Delphi*, home of Apollo, became the religious centre of all Greece. For advice about the future, whether or not a city should go to war, build a temple, found a new colony or make peace, men consulted the *oracle* at Delphi. After suitable gifts and offerings, an answer to the question was given by a drugged priestess whose strange words were interpreted by the temple priests.

Sculpture of a Greek athlete about to throw a discus

THE GAMES

The Greeks admired athletic skill so much that religious festivals were accompanied by athletic meetings in honour of the gods. There were many of these Games, but the greatest were the Olympic Games, held every four years at Olympia in honour of Zeus. A truce was declared between any quarrelling states, so that every city could take part. After prayers and sacrifices, the Games opened with horse and chariot races watched by thousands of spectators on the slopes of the hill of Chronos. The greatest event was the pentathlon, with contests in running, jumping, wrestling and throwing the discus and the javelin. The winner was acclaimed as the best athlete in Greece.

A foreign king supervises the unloading of Greek merchandise from a ship

10. SPARTA, ATHENS AND THE PERSIAN WAR
THE GROWTH OF THE CITY-STATES

RULE OF THE NOBLES

At first, the Greek city-states were ruled by kings, but gradually kings were ousted, except in Sparta. Nobles, or aristocrats, took the lead and under them (800-600 B.C.), the Greeks gave up piracy and took to trade. They were so successful that they soon rivalled the Phoenicians, who had become the sea-going merchants of the Mediterranean world.

SEA-TRADE

In exchange for pottery, wines, oil, honey and fine woollen cloth the Greek merchants brought back grain, amber, silver, hides and timber.

Very early Greek pottery, with fantastic animal designs

The Ionians, busy and alert, quickly learnt to use Asiatic coins and to improve upon them. The Babylonian mina, or pound, of silver was divided, not into sixty parts called shekels, but into 100 parts each called a *drachma*, meaning a " handful," because its value was equal to a handful of small copper rods used for change.

COLONIES

The nobles proved to be harsh rulers, and many Greeks left their homes to found new towns or " colonies " across the sea. They still thought of themselves as Greeks belonging to their parent-city. There were many Greek colonies along the coasts of Asia Minor and the Black Sea, and others in Egypt and North Africa.

Some settlers turned to the unknown West and founded settlements in Sicily and Italy.

A candidate for election to the Council speaks in the open-air to his fellow citizens

THE AGE OF TYRANTS

The nobles made themselves rich at the expense of poorer farmers, but they frequently quarrelled. Then, one noble more powerful than the others would gain the upper hand and become sole ruler. These rulers of the cities were known as " Tyrants," though this does not mean that they were all bad men. Many tyrants were wise rulers who encouraged trade, learning and the arts.

DEMOCRACY

If the tyrants were harsh, or if a good ruler was followed by weak sons, some Greek cities overthrew them.

Then the citizens, meeting in the market-place, chose a Council to manage their affairs, and also a large number of jurors to take turns in trying cases in the law courts. They elected their leaders after hearing them speak in the open air. If they disliked a leading citizen, they banished him.

This manner of rule was possible in small cities where all the freemen could meet together in one place. It was called *democracy*, which means " rule of the people," and has come to be thought of as the best kind of government for men who prize freedom.

SPARTA AND ATHENS

The rivalry between the powerful city-states of Athens and Sparta is an important part of the story of Ancient Greece and, in the end, it brought about the fall of them both.

Two Greek athletes wrestling

Spartan youths in training

The Spartans were descendants of the fierce Dorian tribesmen and they had never mixed with the conquered people of the plain of Laconia. They made them work as *helots*, or slaves, tilling the soil and, on occasions, fighting in the army.

Overlords in the midst of a hostile population, the Spartans had to be ready at a moment's notice to defend their beloved city and its land.

THE CITY

The city itself was little more than a group of straggling villages. It had no fine houses, temples or public buildings because the Spartans despised such things. There was not even a wall round the city, for the Spartans believed that they would fight more bravely without such protection.

At seven years of age a Spartan boy was sent to live in a boarding-school.

He went barefoot and had little food or comfort. He learned to read and write, but most of his time was spent in marching, drilling and sword-play. He was taught to endure cold, to swim icy rivers, to run, box, wrestle and climb mountains. So little food was given him that he was expected to steal cunningly from the tables and gardens of the men's clubs. If he succeeded he was praised, but if he was caught he was flogged.

Sometimes, as part of their training, the boys were encouraged to kill a few helots. This taught them to act cruelly, and it also prevented the slaves from becoming too numerous.

Girls were not taken from their homes, but they, too, were trained to run and jump, to bear pain and cold without complaining so that they would grow up to be strong mothers of warlike sons.

When the boys became men, they continued to live in barracks or clubs and very seldom went home. At marriage, a citizen received a farm but he only visited his wife and children occasionally.

A Council of Elders ruled the city with two kings, one to lead the army in war and the other to act as chief priest. This arrangement prevented either king from becoming too powerful.

The birth of Athena, who sprang fully armed from the head of her father Zeus

ATHENS

Although she was only one of many Greek cities, Athens was the centre of all that is admired in Greek life.

The Athenians, descended from the Ionians, were quick-witted, lively and artistic. They passionately loved their city, and they were devoted equally to freedom and to money-making. In every way opposed to the Spartans, they welcomed new ideas, science, mathematics, music and poetry. They enjoyed public-speaking and argument, so that, later, an important part of the education of young men was to sit round a wise teacher discussing difficult subjects.

A people like this took naturally to trade. Under the leadership of wise rulers Greek trade prospered. Pisistratus, a " tyrant " who died in 527 B.C., imported corn from the Black Sea, and opened gold and silver mines. He also began to beautify the city with fine buildings.

The sons of Pisistratus did not rule well, and the Athenians set up their democracy, whereby the freeborn citizens elected a Council to rule them. There were, of course, many slaves who had no rights in elections, though they seem to have been better treated than in Sparta.

The Athenians, with their wealth and cleverness, and the Spartans, with their grim military power, became bitter rivals in Greece.

THE PERSIAN THREAT

You may recall how Cyrus, King of Persia, swept across Western Asia until he reached the Mediterranean Sea. Here he found prosperous Greek cities along the coast of Asia Minor, and he added them, with Lydia, the kingdom of wealthy Croesus, to his conquests. The city-colonies had to pay tribute and ships to the Persians.

This map shows the most important towns of Ancient Greece, and also the routes taken by Xerxes' army and navy before they were finally defeated at the battle of Salamis

After the death of Cyrus the Greek colonists revolted against *Darius the Great.* Although Athens came to their aid the colonies were defeated, and Darius determined to punish the people who had helped them. He ordered a slave to say to him three times at dinner every day, " Master, remember the Athenians ! "

THE PERSIAN WAR

Not long afterwards, in 490 B.C., the Persians crossed the sea to Greece and landed at Marathon with a great army. The Athenians sent their finest runner, Pheidippides, to Sparta to ask for help, but the Spartans replied that they were having a religious feast and could not come until after the full moon.

So, on the plain of *Marathon*, the Athenians, helped by only 1,000 men from the little city of Plataea, drew up their ranks against the dreaded Persians. Since the enemy did not attack immediately, the Greeks charged at a run with such ferocity that the Persians were thrown into confusion and forced to retreat to their ships.

Pheidippides, the great runner, having fought all day in the battle, ran all the way to Athens with news of the miraculous victory. He stammered out the tidings and fell dead from exhaustion. A modern Marathon race is run over 26 miles, much the same distance as Pheidippides ran to Athens.

The bridge of boats by which the Persians crossed the Hellespont

THE PERSIANS COME AGAIN

Darius died before he could take revenge for Marathon, but he left the task to his son *Xerxes*.

In Athens *Themistocles* tried to convince the citizens that unless they could defeat the Persians at sea they would never be safe. At last a fleet of 200 triremes, warships with three banks of oars, was built at Piraeus.

Xerxes had an army of specially picked soldiers from many conquered nations, with horses, pack-animals, infantry and archers. They were, however, a slave army, driven into battle by whips, whereas the Greeks were defending their own soil.

To cross the narrow channel called the Hellespont, the Persians made a bridge of boats on which brushwood and earth were laid to make a road.

There was even a fence to prevent nervous horses plunging into the waves. Over this bridge passed the soldiers and animals, watched by Xerxes from a lofty throne.

The Persian fleet skirted the coast as the host advanced through northern Greece towards Athens. Heralds were sent into the Greek cities demanding their submission, and it is said that the Spartans gave their answer by throwing the Persian messenger down a well.

Xerxes watches the crossing of the Hellespont

The battle in the pass at Thermopylae

THE BATTLE OF THERMOPYLAE

The Persian army reached *Thermopylae*, a narrow pass between the mountains which was guarded by a Greek army from several cities, including Corinth, Thebes and Phocia, with 300 Spartans. The Spartans had again found an excuse for not sending their army away from the city, and had sent only this small force under their king *Leonidas*.

Spies reported to Xerxes that the Spartans were undismayed by the size of his army, and were combing their hair and doing exercises before the battle.

In the narrow pass the huge Persian numbers were of little avail and the Greeks beat off their attacks. Then a traitor showed the Persians a path over the mountains which would allow them to take the Greeks in the rear. The main body of the Greeks withdrew, but the Spartans and a few others stayed to fight. They fought the entire Persian host, and when Leonidas was killed, they made their stand on a hillock.

Here they fought on with teeth and nails when their swords were broken, until the last man fell beside his comrades.

This battle at Thermopylae is one of the most heroic stands in history. Afterwards, a memorial was put up which simply said, " Stranger, bear word to the Spartans that we lie here obedient to their laws."

A Spartan soldier of the fifth century B.C.

The battle in the Bay of Salamis

THE BATTLE OF SALAMIS

Despite the bravery of the small Spartan force, Athens was doomed. Themistocles decided to abandon the city, and ordered the women and children to be taken to nearby islands, while the men entered the ships in the Bay of Salamis.

From their ships the Athenians watched the Persians capture their beloved city and burn it to the ground.

Themistocles knew that the best way to defeat the Persians would be to fight them at sea in the Bay of *Salamis*, where they would not have room to use their superior numbers.

Secretly he sent a messenger to the Persian fleet saying that the Greeks were about to sail away. As he hoped, they sailed into the bay to meet the Greek ships head-on.

The battle that followed was the first great sea-fight in history. The Greeks had the advantage of being experienced sailors, whereas the Persian ships were filled with unwilling landsmen whose navigators were captive Phoenicians, Ionians and Egyptians. The Athenian ships rammed and sank many of the enemy ships, whose crews were drowned in hundreds.

As the Athenians drove the Persians back, confusion and panic increased among the crowded ships. The battle went on all day, and at the end the Persian fleet was almost wiped out.

This battle, and another victory for the Athenian fleet, drove the Persians from Greek soil, and they never came back again.

The Acropolis of Athens, with the Parthenon to the right

11. THE GOLDEN AGE

THE GREATNESS OF ATHENS

We now come to the most glorious period of Greek history, when vast trading success and wise leadership brought prosperity to Athens and many other cities, especially Corinth.

In Athens a brilliant and handsome young man named Pericles became the leading citizen. He made up his mind to follow the plans of Themistocles to make Athens the greatest and most beautiful city in Greece.

THE ACROPOLIS

In the middle of Athens is the Acropolis, a steep rock rising almost sheer above the surrounding city. Once it had been the fortress of the earliest settlers, but for long it had been the sacred hill for the temples of the gods. The Persians left the temples in ruins and Pericles decided to rebuild them with a magnificence never known before. He was helped by Phidias, the greatest sculptor who ever lived.

Pericles

64

The Acropolis was especially sacred to Athena. Her statue stood at the head of the steps beyond the colonnade leading to the top of the rock.

This statue, designed by Phidias and made of bronze taken from the Persians, stood seventy feet high, looking across the city. Sailors coming home in their ships could see from afar a twinkle of light as the sun flashed on the gilded helmet and spear tip of their goddess.

THE PARTHENON

The Parthenon, much of which is still standing, was the greatest temple in Greece. It stood alone, magnificent, where it could be seen by every citizen, looking upwards as he went about his daily concerns.

Its lovely fluted columns of marble supported a roof which sheltered the shrine of the goddess. Phidias and his pupils made the figures which filled the pediments, or triangular gables, at each end of the roof. They also made the wonderful carved frieze which ran round the upper walls.

In the shrine was a second statue of Athena, carved by Phidias in wood and sheathed in gold and ivory. Every four years a new, costly robe was woven and embroidered by the maidens of Athens and put on this statue. The robe was carried in procession through the city amid great rejoicing.

L.A.H.—E

The temple of Nike, the winged goddess of victory, as it appears today

Phidias was the most famous sculptor, but there were many others whose graceful statues of gods, heroes and athletes adorned the city.

The Statue of the Goddess Athena

Citizens in the Pnyx

THE CITY

Athens had a special assembly place called the Pnyx, an open space where the citizens sat on the ground to listen to speeches and then to vote on important matters.

The market-place (Agora) was surrounded by colonnaded walks with shops behind, while the market-stalls were in the centre. Here the household slaves, not the wives, bought fruit, chickens, honey, vegetables and eggs from the country.

Close by were the law-courts and the public buildings, but these, unlike the temples, were built of sun-dried brick or rubble. Marble was reserved for the gods.

An important building was the Gymnasium, where men took exercises and met their friends.

THEATRES

Music and acting played an important part in the lives of the Greeks, and most cities of any size possessed an open-air theatre. At Athens there was a large theatre at the foot of the Acropolis.

Shopping in the Agora, or market-place, in ancient Athens

Plays developed from dancing and were performed on a flat space called the *orchestra*, from the Greek word meaning *dance*. In time, a wooden stage was added.

A Greek theatre

The chorus, with their graceful dances and chanted songs, were an important part of every play, adding beauty as well as bringing out the meaning of the action. The actors wore masks and wigs, to make the characters clear to a large audience watching in strong sunlight.

At first the audience sat on grassy banks surrounding the orchestra; then wooden benches were added and marble seats for the richer citizens.

As many as 17,000 are said to have gathered to watch the tragedies of Aeschylus, Sophocles and Euripides, the most famous playwrights, whose works are still performed today.

Later, Aristophanes wrote comedies which made fun of people in his own day.

Scene from a Greek comic play

Houses in a narrow street in a Greek town

HOUSES

The Greeks created beautiful temples for their gods and admired the splendid statues which adorned their cities, but they cared little about home life. For most of the year the warm, sunny climate allowed them to work, to enjoy themselves and to meet their friends in the open air. Home was for women and children, a place to eat and sleep in.

Inside a Greek house

Houses built of sun-dried bricks were huddled in narrow, winding streets that had neither gutters nor pavements. There were no windows looking on to the street, but only a door which led into a courtyard open to the sky. Here was the family altar and a shallow pool for rainwater.

Some houses had a well in the courtyard, but usually women slaves went with their tall jars to the public fountain.

There was a verandah with elegant columns round the courtyard, where the family could sit out, shielded from the sun. Several rooms led off the verandah, a dining-room, bedrooms and a kitchen where food was cooked on a raised hearth over small charcoal fires. Bread was cooked in a pottery oven, after hot wood ashes had been raked to one side.

Where there was an upper storey to the house, a staircase led to the women's rooms above.

The inner walls of the house were plastered and painted. Well-to-do homes had mosaic floors, but elsewhere the floors were made of concrete or beaten earth.

FURNITURE

Though the Greeks lived simply, many homes possessed handsome furniture. The chief pieces were couches on which the men reclined at meals.

Women were not expected to use the couches, but there were stools and chairs, seated with leather thongs, which had a very modern appearance. Food was served on low three-legged tables which afterwards could be pushed away under the couches.

Chests were used to store clothes and family possessions, while the women had various small boxes for their trinkets and beauty aids.

There were no cupboards, and musical instruments, such as the seven-stringed lyre, were hung on nails against the walls.

Sappho, a Greek poetess, holding her kythara, *which is played by plucking the strings with the plectrum which she holds in her right hand*

POTTERY

Of all Greek craftsmanship none was more lovely than the pottery. Ordinary pots and jars of the kitchen were beautifully shaped ; there were tall jars for storing wine, water pitchers with a handle to lift them shoulder-high, slim oil jars and scent bottles, drinking cups with twin handles, wine-coolers, flasks and bottles. Some of the largest jars for liquids were sharply pointed at the end, for they were made to stand by being thrust into the earth.

While the ordinary kitchen pots were usually undecorated, most jars in everyday use were decorated with a skill which had never been surpassed. Purple and black patterns were painted in bands round the jars, but the finest vases had human and godlike figures painted in black varnish on a reddish background. Later, the fashion was reversed, and the figures were red on a black background. The drawings were astonishingly lively and they tell us much that we know of life in Ancient Greece.

Greek vases. Those on the left and right are called amphorae, *and were used for storing liquids; the one in the middle is a* kylix, *and was used as a drinking cup*

Women playing knucklebones

PEOPLE IN ATHENS

The well-to-do citizens owned land outside the city, and probably had trading interests too. There were a great many skilled craftsmen as well as labourers, who may have been either freemen or slaves.

In Athens all freeborn citizens, rich or poor, had a share in the government and a vote in the election of their military commander. This gave them a feeling of service towards their city, so that it became quite common for a private citizen to pay for the fitting-out of a warship or for the training of the chorus in a play. He would do this simply for the good of his city.

Slavery was looked upon as a necessity to enable freemen to pursue the arts of civilized living. In Athens, there was a large class of slaves, from the clever craftsmen and scribes, who were well-treated, and the house-slaves who performed all the menial tasks, to the lowest class who toiled in chains in the quarries and silver mines.

CHILDREN

As the house had no garden, children played in the courtyard. Knuckle-bones, ball, pick-a-back, tops and hoops were popular games.

Girls did not go to school but boys were taken there by an old slave called a " pedagogue." He took them to the house of their teacher, where they learned to read and write, to play a musical instrument and to say by heart passages from Homer.

At eighteen an Athenian boy became a citizen and promised to defend his country and obey the laws. He spent a year or two in military training, and then, if his family was well-to-do, he attended the academy for training in athletics, boxing, wrestling and chariot-racing.

Knucklebones   *Dice*

Socrates teaching and talking with his pupils in Athens

TEACHERS AND PHILOSOPHERS

One of the most famous teachers and thinkers was *Socrates*, who liked to teach by asking difficult questions about how men should behave. The elders believed that he was leading the young men to mock the gods, and Socrates was sentenced to death. Though he could have fled, he refused to disobey the law and calmly drank poison and died.

Plato and *Aristotle* were two great thinkers who lived after Socrates. The power of Athens was waning and she was in dire trouble, but they continued to teach that men must be free and must think for themselves.

WOMEN

In Athens women took no part in the affairs of the city, nor did they join their husbands at feasts and entertainments. A woman's place was the home, and, since she usually had slaves to do all the housework and to look after her children, she had to occupy herself with weaving and embroidery, and with gossip about clothes and beauty preparations.

DOCTORS

The Greeks surpassed the Egyptians and became the greatest doctors of ancient times. They tried to discover how the body worked and to cure illness without magic. Of course, they paid some attention to pleasing *Asclepius*, the god of healing; sacrifices and prayers would be made to him before the patient was treated and it was thought helpful if the sick man slept in the skin of a sacrificed ram. *Hippocrates* is the greatest name in Greek medicine, and our doctors still take an Oath which is said to be based upon the oath of service which Hippocrates laid down for doctors.

A carpenter at work with his adze   *A surgeon dresses the arm of one*   *A shoemaker cutting leather for a*
of his patients   *new pair of shoes*

THE FALL OF ATHENS

Pericles, in his desire to make Athens great, subdued many smaller cities and took away their freedom.

They began to look to Sparta to help them to throw off the Athenian yoke, for Sparta, as well as Corinth, was already jealous of the wealth and power of Athens.

War broke out between Athens and Sparta. It is known as the *Peloponnesian War*, and it lasted, on and off, for twenty-six years.

The Athenians were supreme on the sea and the Spartans almost unbeatable on land. Hence it was difficult for either side to deal a knock-out blow.

The Spartans, commanded by Lysander, at last took to the sea and raised a fleet with the help of their allies. The Athenian navy was captured and, in 404 B.C., the proud city surrendered to the Spartans.

THE FALL OF SPARTA

The Greek cities soon found that they had only exchanged one master for a harsher one. They hated the Spartans and despised them for accepting Persian help to defeat Athens.

Thebes, a city to the north of Athens, took the lead against Sparta, and the Theban general *Epaminondas* defeated the Spartan army in two battles and broke her power over the other cities.

Just when it seemed that the Greeks must at last unite, or fall under the power of Persia, a new enemy appeared in the north, where Greece bordered on Macedonia. Too late, Athens realized that *Philip of Macedon* was a soldier-king of genius. The Greeks were defeated at the battle of *Chaeronea* (338 B.C.) and Philip became the master of all Greece except Sparta, which had somewhat recovered her strength.

Greek coin showing the head of Athena

PEOPLE AND EVENTS
TO REMEMBER

The other side of the coin, showing an owl and an olive branch; these designs were often used on Greek coins

B.C.	
about 1500	Minoan civilization in Crete
	Achaeans settled in Greece
„ 1400	Destruction of Knossos
„ 1200	Siege of Troy
„ 1100	Dorians invaded Greece
„ 900	Homer writing poems
800–600	Rise of the city-states
600–500	Age of the Tyrants
492	Darius of Persia invaded Greece
	Themistocles, leader of Athens
490	Persians repulsed at Marathon
480	Xerxes invaded Greece
	Leonidas and his Spartans at Thermopylae
	Sea battle of Salamis

461–431	Pericles and Phidias rebuild Athens
	The Golden Age
	Peloponnesian war
420	Socrates teaching
405	Athens surrendered to Sparta
362	Epaminondas of Thebes beat Sparta
360	Plato in Athens
338	Philip of Macedon defeated the Greeks
356–323	Alexander the Great
334	Battle of Granicus
333	Battle of Issus, Persia overrun
327	Alexander in India
323	Death of Alexander at Babylon

A mourner, with her himation draped over her head as a sign of grief

An elaborate hairstyle of high-born Greek men in the sixth century B.C.

A helmet with a vizor which could be pushed up and down

The hair-style of a young Greek athlete, fifth century B.C.

A helmet with hinged cheek-pieces; the front of the face was left unprotected

73

The Macedonian phalanx

PART FOUR : ALEXANDER THE GREAT

12.   MACEDONIA AND GREECE

THE MACEDONIAN ARMY

The Macedonians were a sturdy peasant race who for a short time became the best soldiers in the world through the genius of Philip and his son, Alexander.

Macedonian infantry, armed with longer, heavier pikes than those of the Greek soldiers, were trained to fight in a dense formation called a *phalanx*. The soldiers formed up in files sixteen-deep, with a space of three feet between each man and the one behind him. The pikes were of great length, no less than twenty-one feet. The first man in each file, a picked soldier, held his pike horizontally with both hands about six feet from one end, where it was made to balance. The next four men behind him did the same, so that the enemy was faced with a five-fold hedge of spear-tips. The remaining men in each file slanted their pikes in the air above the leaders, to parry arrows and to fill any gaps in the ranks.

Lighter troops for skirmishing and shield-bearers, armed with the one-handed pike, made up the rest of the infantry. On either wing were the heavy and the light cavalry. The Macedonians were natural horsemen, but Philip trained them to fight as disciplined cavalry, in support of the infantry. Yet the core of the army was the terrible Macedonian phalanx. When it moved into attack, its irresistible charge swept the enemy before it.

ALEXANDER'S UPBRINGING

Having defeated the Greeks, Philip was still establishing his rule over the city-states, when he was murdered at a wedding-feast. His son, Alexander, twenty years old, succeeded him.

When Alexander was a boy, his father had summoned to court Aristotle, the great philosopher. From him the young prince learned to love Greek ideas and literature, especially the poems of Homer. Handsome, brave and athletic, Alexander believed that he was descended from Hercules and, through his mother, from Achilles. Thus, he became filled with a burning ambition to win fame as a heroic, godlike figure who would lead Greece to wider glory.

ALEXANDER SUBDUES GREECE

At Philip's death the Greek states thought that they would easily throw off the rule of so young a king. But, when the Thebans revolted, Alexander acted with the swiftness for which he was soon to be famous. He captured Thebes and razed it to the ground. Its inhabitants were sold into slavery and their possessions given away. Only the temples and the house of the poet Pindar were spared.

In the face of this ruthlessness the rest of Greece, except Sparta, submitted to Alexander. He at once

Aristotle teaches the young Alexander

began to organize an army of Greeks and Macedonians to fight the Persians, whose empire stretched from Egypt almost to India. During these preparations, Alexander took pains to win the support and admiration of the Greeks by posing as their champion.

The Macedonians conquer Greece

Alexander in battle with his soldiers

THE FIRST VICTORIES

In the spring of 334 B.C. Alexander crossed into Asia. He was never to return.

First, he paused to worship at Troy, to show his reverence for the ancient heroes of Greece. Then he faced the Persian army which was strengthened by a large force of hired Greek soldiers. At the battle of *Granicus*, when Greek fought against Greek, Alexander plunged into the thick of the fighting and led his army to

Alexander reaches Egypt

complete victory. He himself would have been killed but for the timely action of Clitus, son of one of Philip's officers.

In the following year he won an even greater victory at *Issus*, where he smashed the main Persian army under King Darius III, who fled from the field and did not stop until he was east of the Euphrates.

At this point Alexander could have halted and returned home in triumph. Darius offered him all lands west of the Euphrates. His father's old general, Parmenio, urged him to accept the treaty, but Alexander would have none of it. His vision of himself astride the world would not allow him to share it with any man.

EGYPT TAKEN

Alexander now turned south to free the Greek city-colonies and to capture the Phoenician seaports. Syria was conquered, Jerusalem entered, and the way to Egypt lay open.

The Egyptians welcomed Alexander as a god-like deliverer from Persian tyranny. He met no resistance, but stayed long enough to found a great port at the mouth of the Nile, named Alexandria after him.

Alexander receives the tribute of Indian princes

THE OVERTHROW OF PERSIA

Leaving Egypt, Alexander now struck at the heart of Persia. At *Arbela,* in one of the decisive battles of the world, the Greek-Macedonian army met and slaughtered the Persians, whose host was said to amount to a million men. Darius III again fled and was later murdered by one of the few officers who remained with him. The power of Persia was broken.

Babylon surrendered without a blow ; Susa and Persepolis, treasure cities of the Persian Empire, fell into Alexander's hands with their fabulous stores of silver and gold. At Persepolis Alexander himself set fire to the vast palaces, the most magnificent buildings ever erected in the East.

He did this to avenge the burning of Athens by Xerxes, and perhaps to show that it was his hand that had destroyed Persia's might. Afterwards he is known to have regretted this deed.

TO INDIA

Leaving the trusty old general Parmenio in charge of the treasure, Alexander now led his army farther and farther east.

In 327 B.C., he came down into the great plains of India itself, where most of the princes submitted to him. Restless as ever, he determined to cross the River Ganges and press into the heart of India, when at long last his weary soldiers refused to march.

Unwillingly, for he never forgave them, Alexander yielded to his soldiers' wishes. Sailing down the Indus, he founded another Alexandria at its mouth, where he gazed with wonder at the tides of the Indian Ocean. Then he led the army homeward along the coast and across mountain ranges while his admiral Nearchus, in a newly built fleet, was ordered to explore the mysterious sea.

Alexander kills Clitus

After great hardships and the loss of many men through exhaustion and thirst, Alexander reached Babylon again.

ALEXANDER'S CHANGED CHARACTER

Complete power and astounding success had turned Alexander's natural pride into cruel vanity. Suspicions of old friends led to the execution of faithful Parmenio and his son. Enraged by criticism, Alexander snatched a spear at a feast and killed Clitus, who had saved him in battle. More and more he resembled an Eastern monarch, before whom even his closest comrades must kneel and kiss his feet.

ALEXANDER'S PLANS

Lord of the ancient world, and still interested in art, science and literature, Alexander planned to rule a vast empire united by the Greek language and civilization.

He busied himself with a hundred projects. Expeditions were despatched to explore the Upper Nile and the Caspian Sea. Plans were made to conquer the countries of the Western Mediterranean by building a colossal road along the coast of North Africa.

In 323 B.C., Alexander, preparing an expedition to conquer Arabia, made a river trip down the Euphrates. On his return to Babylon he became ill with marsh-fever. Ten days later his Macedonian veterans were allowed to file past his bedside to bid farewell to their general. That afternoon Alexander the Great died. He was thirty-two years old. His reign had lasted only twelve years and eight months.

His vast empire was divided between his generals, and after many struggles three kingdoms emerged, Syria, Egypt and Greece.

Alexander's soldiers file past his bed to bid farewell as he lies dying

PART FIVE: THE STORY OF ROME

14. THE BUILDING OF ROME

THE SITE OF ROME

Roman children were taught that when the Greeks captured Troy a man named *Aeneas* escaped with his father, his little son and a few companions. They set sail and came at last to the plain of Latium, in Italy. Here, Aeneas married the king's daughter and founded a kingdom.

Romulus and Remus found by the wolf

Years later, his descendant, King Numitor, was driven out by his brother. Numitor's daughter had twin sons, named *Romulus* and *Remus*, whom the wicked uncle ordered to be thrown into the River Tiber. But the babies were washed ashore and cared for by a she-wolf, until a shepherd rescued them. When the boys grew up they won back their father's kingdom and decided to build a new city for themselves.

and finished the wall alone. Thus, the city was called Rome, after Romulus, its first king. Legend said that Rome was founded in the year 753 B.C.

Whether this story is true or not, it is certain that, at about this time, a straggling settlement grew up on the seven hills overlooking a point where the Tiber could be crossed.

THE CITY ON SEVEN HILLS

Romulus chose a place on the southern bank of the Tiber where seven little hills made a natural strong-point. On the Palatine Hill he was beginning to build his wall when a quarrel broke out between the brothers. Romulus killed Remus

The position was a good one for defence and for trade. Gradually the uncultured farmer-settlers began to prosper, but they had to fight constantly against neighbouring peoples who were jealous of their growing power.

79

THE ITALIAN TRIBES

Before the rise of Rome, there were several separate tribes inhabiting the country. Most of them had entered Italy from the north and, like the Greeks, to whom they were closely related, had seized lands and had settled down to a simple way of life.

They did not, however, find a civilization which they could copy and improve upon, as the Greeks did.

Rome and the neighbouring tribes in Italy

By sea had come the *Etruscans* to settle just north of the Tiber. They had learned writing and the use of bronze and pottery from the Greeks.

The people of the plain of Latium were called *Latins*, and they had made a league with the little town of Rome to fight against the powerful Etruscans.

In the mountains lived the *Umbrians* and in central Italy were the energetic *Samnites*.

Etruscan earrings and a necklace worked in gold

In the toe of Italy and in Sicily were *Greek City-colonies*, whose rich, civilized citizens, busy with trade and their own affairs, had no interest in the struggles of the rough farming people to the north.

An Etruscan mask used in funeral rites, with magic designs intended to keep evil spirits away

An Etruscan soldier's helmet

An Etruscan hand-mirror

ROME FIGHTS WARS

The Romans learned much from their neighbours the Etruscans across the river. They learned how to use the arch in their buildings, and they also learned the alphabet, which, little altered, we use today.

The Etruscans were probably Rome's overlords for a time, but the Romans, helped by their Latin allies, fought valiantly for their freedom. After many years, they managed to capture the Etruscan city of Veii and to add all their enemy's lands to their own.

Then another foe appeared. The barbarian Gauls had settled in the valley of the Po, which was not then considered part of Italy. These fierce tribesmen destroyed outlying farms and, in 390 B.C., captured and burnt Rome itself. They could not capture the Capitol, the fortress on a hill where stood the temple of Jupiter and Juno. Here a band of Romans held out for months. One night, the Gauls found a secret path up the steep cliff on one side of the hill. In single file, the Gauls almost reached the top, when Juno's sacred geese began to cackle in alarm. This aroused the garrison who hurled back the enemy and the Capitol was saved. Soon afterwards, the Gauls retired from the city, but all its early history had been destroyed in the fire and only legends, like that of Romulus and Remus, remained.

Juno's geese give warning of the approach of the Gauls

Elephants used in battle

ROME CONQUERS ALL ITALY

After she had defeated the Etruscans and Gauls, Rome was able to turn her attention to the south. First she subdued her Latin allies and then the *Samnites*, a brave hill-people who put up a stubborn struggle.

A handle for the lid of a box, made from models of three Etruscan soldiers

Only the rich Greek cities remained. Realizing their danger, they asked help from *Pyrrhus*, King of Epirus in Greece.

Pyrrhus was a relation of Alexander the Great, and he brought over to Italy an army which included cavalry, elephants and the Macedonian phalanx. The Romans were defeated in several battles, but their spirit never flagged. Fresh troops took the place of those who had died, while the army of Pyrrhus grew ever smaller. He declared that he could not afford to win any more victories of this kind and eventually he returned to his own country.

Lacking a general of the quality of Pyrrhus, the Greek cities of southern Italy gave up the struggle. The last to surrender was the great seaport of Tarentum, and, in the year 272 B.C., after 200 years of fighting, Rome was mistress of the whole of Italy.

WAR WITH CARTHAGE

Almost at once, Rome had to grapple with the mightiest foe she had yet encountered.

Carthage, standing on a headland of North Africa, was the greatest merchant city of the world. Carthaginian seamen not only traded throughout the Mediterranean, but ventured through the Pillars of Hercules out on to the Atlantic Ocean and northwards as far as the tin islands of Britain.

The Romans were not a seafaring race but, with their genius for war, they set about defeating the Carthaginians by sea as well as on land.

They built a fleet and invented a secret weapon, called the " corvus " (crow), which was a wooden bridge with a great spike at one end. When alongside the enemy, the corvus was dropped on to the opponent's deck ; the spike held the two ships together and the Romans poured across the wooden bridge and fought hand to hand.

After a long time, in 241 B.C., the Carthaginians were driven out of Sicily. A new Carthaginian army of hired soldiers was commanded by *Hannibal*. Though only twenty-four years old, he was a general to rank with Alexander and Caesar, and he formed a plan to take the Romans by surprise.

He marched his army, which included cavalry and elephants, through

Roman soldiers board an enemy ship by means of a corvus

Spain, along the Mediterranean coast and into Italy through the Alps. No one believed that an army could cross those vast mountains. It was nearly winter ; snowstorms hindered the march but, in the teeth of cold, hunger and incessant attacks by mountain tribes, Hannibal led his men through the passes and down into the plains of Italy.

Hannibal's army marches over the Alps

Hannibal

He completely defeated the Romans three times, but, great general though he was, he could not deal Rome a death-blow. Because of the Roman success at sea Carthage could send him no more troops, and his army was too small to besiege the city of

Rome. For fifteen years he kept up the struggle in Italy, while the Romans, not daring to meet him in open battle, recovered their strength. At last Hannibal returned to Africa, where, at *Zama*, in 202 B.C., he was defeated by *Scipio*, a brilliant Roman general. Carthage was forced to ask for peace.

THE END OF CARTHAGE

Rome's strength seemed unending, for she now punished those who had helped Carthage. Philip V of Macedon was overcome and Greece was added to Rome's possessions. Soon afterwards, most of Asia Minor fell into her power.

Cato, the orator

But Carthage, left alone, began to grow rich again. There were Romans who never forgot how near they had been to defeat, and they were certain that Rome could never be safe while Carthage existed. A certain statesman named Cato always ended a speech with the words " Carthage must be destroyed." So, in 146 B.C. when war flared up again, the Romans took Carthage, killing or capturing all its inhabitants. Brick by brick, they tore down the city and finally they ploughed up the very ground on which the city stood. No trace of Carthage remained.

The election of a Consul

15. THE REPUBLIC

THE GOVERNMENT OF THE REPUBLIC

At first Rome had been ruled by kings, with the help of a council of old men called the Senate.

There were seven kings, but the last, *Tarquin the Proud*, was so harsh that he was driven from the city. The hated name of king (" rex ") was never used again, and Rome became a republic.

Instead of a king, two magistrates, called *consuls*, were chosen to rule the city for a period of one year. They wore the toga with a purple stripe, and their attendants carried a bundle of rods with an axe in the middle. This showed their power to give punishment by beating and death, and the bundle became the sign of Roman rule.

The Senate still met to give advice, and the citizens, meeting in the Assembly, elected the two consuls for their year of leadership.

PATRICIANS AND PLEBEIANS

Roman citizens were divided into two classes ; the patricians were rich nobles and the plebeians were poorer farmers and workers. Only patricians could become consuls or enter the Senate. Even in the Assembly, the patricians had control of the votes, so, in truth, the plebeians had little share in ruling the city.

For more than 100 years there was a bitter and often bloodthirsty struggle between patricians and plebeians. In the end the plebeians gained the right to elect two officers called " tribunes of the people " who looked after the interests of the ordinary citizens.

EVERYDAY LIFE IN ROME

A Roman farmer-citizen ploughs his land

Unlike the Greeks, he was not fond of talking about government in the market-place, nor of athletic exercise.

He had no particular ability as a trader nor a great love of beautiful things. He was neither craftsman nor artist, but he believed that his duty was to be brave and loyal to Rome, to his family and the gods.

A ROMAN OF THE EARLY REPUBLIC

When, from a mean little town surrounded by a few miles of farmland, Rome was growing to power, the citizen lived a simple, hard-working life.

He worked on his farm, and, even when he grew richer he still busied himself in seeing that his servants and slaves carried out their tasks.

Inside a Roman house

AN EARLY HOME

The Roman in the early days of the Republic lived in a home consisting of one room, the *atrium,* to which he added smaller rooms as his position improved. In the atrium, the family took their meals, entertained friends, cooked the food and worshipped the household gods. The room was open to the sky in the centre, where a square hole in the roof admitted light and air, and allowed the smoke of the fire to escape. The roof sloped inwards, and there was a shallow pool in the floor to catch rainwater.

Furniture and possessions were few ; there would be one or two chests for clothes, some cooking pots and various household jars, probably of Etruscan ware. There were also little statues of the gods of the home, which were the family's most precious possessions.

Roman boys at school. One boy is working his sums by means of an abacus

SCHOOLING

For a long time the Romans had much less interest in education and learning than the Greeks. Boys were taught the " Twelve Tables " of the law, which Romans held in great respect.

Boys were usually taught at home by a tutor from whom they learned reading and writing and, above all, complete obedience to their fathers. From about seven years of age, they attended private schools where they were taught their own language, Latin, and Greek, with the help of a good deal of flogging. Writing was done on wax tablets with the stylus, or on papyrus with a reed pen. Arithmetic was simple compared with Greek mathematics, and consisted mostly of learning how to use the counting frame or *abacus*.

Homer was translated into Latin and long passages had to be learned by heart. Music, medicine and astronomy became important subjects, and much attention was given to rhetoric—the art of public speaking. Roman youths of good family often finished their schooling in Athens, which was still the centre of culture and learning.

Girls were not thought worthy of much education ; they were kept at home, learning how to manage the household, to spin and weave, until they were married, between the early ages of twelve and nineteen.

Writing tablets. These are models of account-books, which were found at Pompeii

Mars   *Minerva*   *Jupiter*   *Diana*

RELIGION

Religion was at the centre of every Roman home, and every family possessed a shrine or altar at which the household gods and the spirit of the hearth and store-cupboard were worshipped. Little images of these spirits were made of clay, ivory, silver or gold according to the householder's wealth, and were most carefully guarded. Prayer was said daily to them and small offerings of food and wine set before their shrine, on which a lamp was always kept burning.

Two important gods of the household were Janus, god of the doorway, from whom we have the name of the month of January, and Vesta, goddess of the hearth or fire, specially tended by the daughters of the house. The temple of Vesta was one of the most ancient in the city and its sacred fire was looked after by six beautiful, well-born maidens, known as the Vestal Virgins.

The Roman gods took on the characters of the Greek deities. Jupiter, whose temple was on the Capitoline Hill, was king of all the gods and Juno, his wife, was the sky-goddess. Here is a list of the Roman gods :

Jupiter	god of light, king of the gods.
Juno	queen of the gods.
Vesta	goddess of the hearth.
Mars	god of war.
Ceres	goddess of the harvest, the earth-mother.
Minerva	goddess of wisdom.
Venus	goddess of love; her little son was Cupid.
Janus	god of the doorway.
Diana	goddess of the moon and of hunting.
Neptune	god of the sea.
Vulcan	god of fire, the blacksmith.
Mercury	messenger of the gods, protector of trade.

Christians in the arena about to be attacked by lions

After the time of Julius Caesar, the emperors were raised to the level of gods and it was the duty of citizens to worship them.

Later, several foreign gods became widely popular; temples to the Egyptian goddess Isis, and to the Persian god of light, Mithras, were set up in widely separated parts of the empire.

CHRISTIANITY IN THE ROMAN REPUBLIC

The readiness to accept foreign gods helped St. Paul to spread the religion of Jesus Christ, who was born in the Roman province of Judea. St. Paul's teaching and the publication of the Gospels in Greek caused Christianity to spread to Rome itself. But the refusal of the Christians to worship the emperor led to horrible persecutions, especially during the reigns of Nero and Diocletian.

However, Christianity went on spreading, and by about A.D. 200 every Roman province had its Christian churches. In A.D. 313 the Emperor Constantine gave permission for Christianity to be recognized with other religions of the Empire, and a little later it became the official religion of the State. Even when Rome collapsed, Christianity survived.

A coin showing the head of Constantine

Poor people from the nearby countryside pillage and set fire to a wealthy farmer's property

THE ROMAN POOR

Side by side with the wealth and luxury of the upper class of Rome there existed a vast number of desperately poor people, whose misery and occasional violence were a danger to the State.

As the poor became angry and troublesome, the rich citizens thought that the way to keep them quiet was to give them free food, and to provide entertainment to fill their idle days.

Because there was cheap corn from conquered lands the small farmers could no longer make a living. Their farms were bought up to make great estates and the country-folk flocked into the city. But here the arrival of cheap slaves made paid work difficult to get. To the numbers of poor countrymen were added hundreds of soldiers back from the wars, and workmen who had lost their jobs to the slaves. Only highly skilled workers, such as jewellers and cooks, could obtain good wages.

Idlers gossip in the Forum at Rome

Chariot-racing in the arena in Rome

THE CIRCUS

Popular leaders provided free " spectacles " or shows which soon became a regular feature of life in Rome and the provincial cities.

Chariot races and athletic meetings were held in the *Circus Maximus*, a huge oval arena, with room for more than 180,000 spectators. The chariot course was nearly a mile long with sharp bends at each end, where the charioteers had to show skill and cunning when cornering at tremendous speed. Their light chariots were drawn by two-, three- and four-horse teams which were bred especially for racing in southern Italy. The charioteers wore, for protection, thongs of leather round their bodies and thighs, and they carried a curved knife so that in a collision they could slash free the reins that were fastened round their waists.

The chariot-races caused enormous excitement and furious betting, and

it was not long before the unruly crowds demanded shows that were even more exciting.

A charioteer. He has his curved knife tucked into the thongs of leather which are bound round his body

Gladiators in the arena

Emperors and ambitious patricians provided fights between gladiators. In these contests armed men, called *gladiators*, fought to the death in the arena. The gladiators were criminals, slaves, prisoners of war and, occasionally, volunteers, who were trained in special barracks and given massage and exercise like modern professional boxers. The most popular contest was between a lightly built man armed with a net, dagger and trident, and an opponent equipped with sword and shield.

When a man was wounded after fighting well, the audience would wave their handkerchiefs or turn up their thumbs to allow him mercy, but if they had not liked his performance, they turned down their thumbs as a signal to his opponent to put him to death. Successful gladiators who survived were sometimes given a pension, with a wooden sword as the sign of their honourable retirement.

Wrestling and boxing matches were often followed by wild beast shows, when animals specially brought from North Africa were slaughtered by the hundred. Occasionally, the whole arena was flooded to provide a spectacle with sea-battles between fleets of warships.

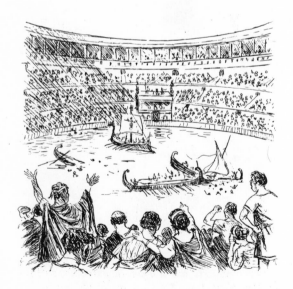

Flooded arena with mock sea-battle

These drawings show how the toga developed in ancient Rome. The two drawings on the left show the simple draping of the early style; the two on the right show the draping of the toga many years later, and the purple band clearly shows the intricate winding of the garment

CLOTHES

The traditional garment of the workers was the *tunic*, a short woollen garment, gathered at the waist by a belt ; workmen often slipped their right arm out of its sleeve to leave the shoulder bare for heavy work. Nobles, and even the emperor himself, sometimes wore linen or silk tunics, embroidered with gold thread. Cloaks were usually made of wool, oblong in shape and fastened by a brooch on the right shoulder. A semi-circular cloak with a hood was worn by both men and women when travelling.

The dignified. dress of well-to-do Romans was the *toga*, a large semi-circular garment worn over a tunic and short drawers.

The toga was usually white or natural wool colour, but youths and magistrates wore togas with a red or purple band along the straight edge. There were black togas for mourning, while victorious generals and, in later days, emperors and consuls, wore the purple toga with gold embroidered stripe. The style of draping the toga became more complicated and it lost its popularity, except for official occasions.

High-laced boots, half-boots which left the toes bare, and boots which fastened with thongs, were made of soft, raw leather, though men of high birth had the leather dyed scarlet. Sandals were worn indoors, but poor men and slaves went barefoot.

Two Roman workmen and, in the middle, a lictor, or attendant on the consul, who carries the fasces, a bundle of rods with an axe in the middle, the sign of Roman rule

The dress of a girl about twelve years old

Hats were seldom worn, though a conical felt cap or a rounded Greek hat was occasionally seen. Though beards were known in the early days of the Republic, and the Emperor Hadrian grew a short beard, the Roman was usually clean-shaven, with short hair, combed down all round his head.

Father, mother, and son in the graceful clothes of the first century A.D.

Hairstyles of the first century A.D.

Roman ladies dressed almost exactly like the Greeks. They wore the chiton or tunic, which was not sewn on the shoulders but fastened with brooches. This flowing garment sometimes had sleeves ; when it was sleeveless the under-tunic had sleeves instead. The tunic was gathered in under the breast and, for matrons, was decorated with a coloured border at the hem of the skirt. A woollen cloak called the *palla* was worn outdoors in a variety of styles, since it was very large and could be wrapped twice round the body and draped over the head like a hood. Ladies wore little boots of soft coloured leather in the street, and light sandals at home.

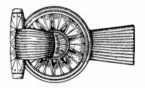

A brooch

A betrothal, or engagement ring

Sandals

Though styles in clothes changed little, Roman ladies spent a great deal of time over their toilet and hair styles ; curls, waves, combs, braids and elaborate plaiting were all fashionable at times. Many aids to beauty, such as rouge, paint, eyebrow-tweezers and manicure sets were everyday possessions of smart Roman matrons.

Boots

Fighting in the streets of Rome

THE END OF THE REPUBLIC

The Romans had always respected law and discipline. That was one reason why their armies were so successful and why Rome was able to rule so vast an empire. But lack of work in Italy, free food and circuses, gave rise to a lazy, discontented class who had no respect for the law.

Slaves were usually harshly treated and on the big estates were chained together like beasts. Many slaves escaped and roamed the country in armed bands, plundering and murdering like small armies.

These unruly times caused men to feel that they needed a strong leader. The Senate was old and the consuls, elected for only a year at a time, had too little time to restore order.

When barbarian tribes from the north threatened the safety of Italy it became necessary for Rome's best general, *Marius*, to be elected consul for six years running so that he could keep command of the army. This not only broke the rule that a consul held office for one year only, but it made Marius the most powerful man in the state.

A short time afterwards another consul named *Sulla* gained great power, and kept it by putting to death all who opposed him.

Soon Rome was divided into two savage parties who fought bitterly for power, so that murders and street-fighting became everyday affairs. At last there arose a man great enough to bring order and peace to the unhappy city. He was Julius Caesar.

Julius Caesar

JULIUS CAESAR

Caesar was a well-educated Roman of good family but no great wealth. He gained popularity by providing bread and circuses for the poor with the help of a rich friend. He became consul and gained command of an army to subdue the barbarian tribes of Gaul (France).

Though he had held no military command until he was forty, Caesar became one of the greatest generals who has ever lived. In a few years he completely overcame the Gauls and added vast lands to Roman rule. It was during this time that he made his famous expeditions to Britain.

His public generosity and his military success gave him a devoted army and when, in 51 B.C., he marched towards Rome, everyone wondered what he would do. Would he give up his command and become a private citizen or would he try to become master of Rome? Breaking the law, Caesar brought his army to the city to overawe the Senate and their leader Pompey. The people of Rome elected him consul again and gave him complete power.

Vercingetorix, a Gaelic chieftain who led a revolt against the Romans, surrenders to Julius Caesar

Julius Caesar is stabbed in the Senate House, at the foot of a statue to Pompey

Caesar now set about overcoming the Senate forces by a series of brilliant campaigns in Spain, Greece, and Asia Minor. After one battle, he sent back to Rome a message of three words—" Veni, vidi, vici," which means " I came, I saw, I conquered." Pompey was defeated and Caesar was free to return to Rome to rule the state wisely and well.

He showed mercy and wisdom in all that he did, laying the foundations of law and government that lasted Rome for centuries, but there were men in Rome who believed that he would set himself up to become a king. He was stabbed to death in the Senate House, and thus died, " the greatest of the Romans."

OCTAVIAN

The murder of Caesar caused civil war to break out, but, after several years, his great-nephew *Octavian* defeated all enemies and gained sole power. It was at this time, when Octavian defeated Mark Antony and Queen Cleopatra, that Egypt became a Roman province.

Octavian became known as Caesar Augustus and, though he never called himself emperor, he was the first of the great rulers of the Empire.

A Roman archway

16. THE ROMAN EMPIRE
THE GOVERNMENT OF THE EMPIRE

The great stone slabs of one of the ancient Roman roads, the Via Flaminia. The modern road runs beside it

The Republic was ended, and from now on the Empire was ruled by one man, the Emperor, aided by numerous governors, magistrates and civil servants.

The Empire was divided into provinces, each ruled by a governor who possessed the powers of a minor emperor. He raised taxes, built towns roads and fortifications, commanded the army, and enriched himself.

Steadily the Empire increased in size as new territories were added, though the time came when Rome wanted no more lands but a wall and a strong series of armies to keep the barbarians in check. One of the later provinces was Britain, a small island on the very edge of the civilized world, which produced tin, hides and corn. It is proof of the wonderful strength of Roman rule that this obscure island became a prosperous province, richly furnished with towns, ports, wealthy villas and a first-class road system.

The Empire was linked together by trade, by the Latin language, and by its splendid roads. " All roads lead to Rome " was a true saying, for the highways so carefully surveyed and laid down by the soldiers were not only military roads along which troops could march at speed, but they were the routes used by Imperial messengers hurrying with orders from the capital, and along which trundled most of the world's wealth and trade.

Building a Roman road

THE ROMAN ARMY

The Romans had fought their way to leadership because their soldiers were better trained, better armed and better disciplined than their opponents.

The backbone of the army was the *legion*, formed of Roman citizens and numbering between 3,000 and 6,000 men. Each legion was divided into ten *cohorts*, and each cohort divided into *centuries*, or companies of 100 soldiers, led by their centurions, upon whom the discipline of the Legion depended.

The legionary wore a metal or leather helmet and a breastplate, with knee-length tunic and short breeches. His boots were hob-nailed, since he was trained to march immense distances. Ordinary soldiers had a brown cloak, officers a white one, and generals scarlet. The officers and centurions wore helmets which bore a plume of red or black feathers.

The foot-soldier carried a curved shield, iron-rimmed and covered with leather, and was armed with a double-edged short sword, a dagger and two seven-foot javelins or throwing-spears. On the march, he carried a heavy pack which included a short spade, a handmill for corn, rations, spare clothes, cooking pot and two wooden stakes for the protection of the camp each night.

A Roman legionary (from Trajan's column)

Centurions carried a stout staff of vine wood as the sign of their rank, just as, in modern armies, senior ranks often carry a cane.

Three Roman soldiers: a legionary, carrying a spear, a centurion, and a Praetorian Guard, one of the Emperor's bodyguard

A standard-bearer

Each cohort also had its *signum*, a pole bearing images and metal discs.

Besides the legionaries, the cream of the army, there were the *Auxiliaries*, consisting of cavalry wings, archers, slingers, dart-throwers and special troops, such as camel-corps and light skirmishers. These auxiliaries were recruited from the provinces, usually in the wilder parts of the Empire, such as Gaul, Germany and Asia.

The silver eagle of the Legion was carried into battle by the Standard-bearer, wearing his lion or leopard-skin about his shoulders. The eagle bore the honour of the legion and its capture was a disaster bringing lasting disgrace and ill-fortune.

The Romans learned to use and improve the Assyrian siege machines and every legion was equipped with artillery. The machines included catapults for hurling heavy stones and javelins, battering-rams, siege-towers and shelters for men undermining walls or storming a breach.

Roman military devices in action

A Roman forum

THE CITY OF ROME

Augustus and the emperors who followed him gave Rome the most magnificent public buildings which any capital has ever possessed. A triumphal arch led into the ancient Forum, or market-place. This was flanked by the temple of Julius Caesar, the Senate-house, and various arches and temples which rose to the Capitol, crowned by the Temple of Jove. Several more magnificent forums were laid out by the emperors. They had imposing buildings such as the theatre of Pompey, the Baths of Agrippa, the Pantheon, a vast building with a colossal dome of concrete, several libraries, and Trajan's Column, which, like several of these columns, still stands today.

Aqueducts, which brought water for the fountains and baths from distant hills, were so well built that some are still in use and remains of many others can be seen in Italy, France and Spain.

A vast Amphitheatre, called the Colosseum, was built by the Emperor Vespasian to seat 50,000 spectators, and its opening was celebrated by games, gladiatorial contests and " spectacles " lasting for 100 days !

The Colosseum in Rome

A street in a Roman town. Notice the cobbled road and the stepping-stones on the street corner

LIFE IN A ROMAN TOWN

Throughout the great empire, innumerable new towns and cities were built, all, to some extent, a small copy of Rome itself.

Each town was carefully planned; there was a wall all round, with towers and gates at regular intervals. Inside, the town was neatly laid out with straight roads crossing at right angles. Near the centre was the forum, or main square, flanked by handsome public buildings, such as the law-courts, council-house, temples of Jupiter, Apollo and other gods. These buildings were made of brick, faced perhaps with marble, but more often plastered and then painted with colourful designs.

The forum was the busiest place in the town. Here, and also in the meat and cloth markets, were to be found noisy, jostling crowds of citizens, businessmen, lawyers and workers, discussing their affairs and carrying out their business in the open air. Slaves made their way through the crowd, carrying goods and the day's shopping for their mistresses at home. Here and there were groups of idlers and workless men, waiting to catch the eye of some important man to gain his favour.

The paved streets of the town were narrow, just wide enough for a two-wheeled cart or chariot, since larger waggons were made to unload at the town gates. Stepping-stones were provided at crossing-places, so that ladies in their fine gowns and light boots could avoid puddles and rubbish.

If the town was of any size and importance, it would contain barracks, both for soldiers and for the gladiators. There was also a prison. The law-abiding citizen could stroll in the public gardens, to admire the fountains and the statues of Hercules.

At the gymnasium he would meet his friends and enjoy the gossip of the day, while an attendant rubbed him with scented oil and scraped his skin with a curved instrument called a *strigil*.

The courtyard or atrium of a house

Near the walls, or just outside, was the arena, and sometimes a theatre as well, at which the governor provided plays, athletic sports and the popular gladiatorial and wild beast shows.

Romans in the gymnasium. The man in the foreground is using his strigil

Roman comedians entertaining their audience. This scene has been done in mosaic by a Roman artist, using hundreds of small stones of varying colours and shades. The mosaic was found at Pompeii

A visitor arrives to seek admittance to a house which is behind the shop shown on the left

HOUSES AND SHOPS

Well-to-do Romans had enlarged their houses by adding, beyond the atrium, a number of rooms, built round a courtyard gay with flower-beds and a fountain or statue. In towns such as Pompeii and Herculaneum the rich lived in comfort and elegance that can hardly be equalled today.

From the street, even a wealthy home looked unimposing, owing to the custom of letting most of the front of the house as a lock-up shop.

The shop was merely a single room, with sometimes a storeroom attached. It faced on to the pavement, so that customers could pause as they walked and examine the goods set out on a stone counter. At night, the shop-keeper put wooden shutters over the opening above the counter, and went off to his home in another part of the town. Though small, the shops sold wares of every kind—bread, fruit, meat, and wine and olive oil in large jars.

The best shops were in the forum and in the streets leading off it, where silversmiths, jewellers, sandal-makers, potters and glass-makers offered goods of wonderful variety and high quality.

Ignoring the shop outside, a visitor to a rich friend knocked at the house door and was admitted to the vesti-bule by the door-keeper. Just inside the house there was probably a

A Roman carving of a butcher in his shop. His scales are behind him, and various cuts of meat—ribs, a shoulder, a pig's head—are hanging from the rail above him. His wife has writing tablets on her knee; perhaps she is checking the accounts

little shrine in the wall or a picture of Janus, god of the doorway.

The visitor now entered the atrium, where he noticed that the walls were newly decorated with paintings of gods and cupids. A staircase led up to bedrooms above, but a house-slave showed him into a little guest-room, off the atrium, where there was a built-in bed of masonry against the wall, and a cheerful picture to amuse him.

Another door from the atrium led to the kitchen, where slaves prepared the meals and the cook fried or boiled the food at a raised cooking stove. On the top of the stove were several shallow holes containing char-coal which the cook fanned into bright heat beneath the cooking pots, which stood above the fire on metal grills. The Romans seldom baked their food, but bought bread and cakes from the baker whose shop was in one of the main streets, with the sign of the god of rich harvests carved on the side of his oven for luck.

Next to the kitchen was the winter dining-room, with glass window-panes, rich wall-paintings of the gods, and beneath the floor and in the walls were flues which carried warm air from a furnace. The floor itself was made of hundreds of small cubes of stone set close together to make a pattern or a picture of great detail. The mosaic worker, usually a slave,

Part of a mosaic from the Temple of Fortune at Palestrina, a town near Rome. The mosaic shows scenes during the flooding of the River Nile

used coloured stones, such as lime-stone and marble, which he cut into cubes by tapping with a hammer against a cutting tool set in a block of wood.

A poor quarter in a Roman town. The houses are crumbling and dirty, and a brawl is about to break out

Leading off the verandah were other rooms, including the summer dining-room, bathroom, lavatory and chapel of the household gods.

In the poorer parts of the town were the workshops of dyers, tanners, carpenters and blacksmiths. Here, too, were blocks of flats and small houses, crowded together in narrow alleys, where the poor lived with few possessions and

From the atrium, the visitor now stepped into an enchanting garden, surrounded by a *peristyle*, or verandah supported by columns. There his host reclined in the shade, while his children and their nurse played knuckle-bones in the sunshine.

little comfort. Their lives were cheered by the excitement of election or of shows in the amphi-theatre, but sometimes their behaviour was so violent that the magistrates would order the arena to be closed as a punishment.

The garden and peristyle of a well-to-do Roman villa

Goths and Vandals

THE DOWNFALL OF ROME

Rome was mistress of the known world, ruling almost all the territories of the older civilizations and many others to the north and west. For several centuries, Rome gave peace, law and order to most of her provinces, though there were often minor troubles, and always danger, along the frontiers. Nevertheless, her citizens and subjects knew safety, prosperity and peace for a longer period than the world has known before or since.

Why did Rome fall? Why did that marvellous organization, with its roads, cities, harbours, its learning, trade and, above all, its invincible legions, collapse, so that in many places hardly a trace of the grandeur was left?

From about A.D. 200, the Empire began slowly to decay from inside. Many of the emperors were cruel and greedy, some were wicked, others were mad. At times, rival emperors, elected by the legions, fought for supremacy. Weak rule from Rome allowed governors in the provinces to get rich quickly by wringing heavy taxes from their subjects. Lawyers and magistrates took bribes, and this weakened respect for Roman justice.

As law and order declined, trade began to suffer, for robbers waylaid merchants on the roads and pirates infested the seas.

CAPTURE OF ROME

As Rome grew weaker within, the barbarians beyond the frontiers grew bolder. Goths and Vandals attacked from the north, Saxon tribes harried the shores of Britain and the Huns from Germany poured into Gaul and Italy.

Byzantine architecture: the Church of St. Sophia in Constantinople, built about the fifth and sixth centuries A.D.

BYZANTIUM

The Roman Empire did not perish altogether when the city of Rome fell. The Emperor Constantine, who became a Christian, had already moved the capital to Byzantium, afterwards Constantinople, at the mouth of the Black Sea. From 330, in this magnificent new city, the emperors continued to rule what was left of their domains in the east. It was only a shadow of Rome's former glory, but Constantinople preserved learning and the arts. Above all, it preserved Christianity, so that when the barbarian tribes finally overran all Rome's lands in the West, turning them into separate countries, the Christian religion was so strongly established that the barbarians respected it and were gradually converted.

Rome itself was sacked and burnt by the Goths in 410, and in 476 German tribes deposed the Emperor.

These fierce barbarians hated and despised civilized living; they swept across the provinces burning and killing wherever they went. Some of them settled down in the lands which they had overrun, to lead the sort of lives they had known in their own countries, primitive and rural. They destroyed the towns and elegant country villas and built small farming settlements with timber-framed hut dwellings in their place. Science, learning, road-making, the arts of building and commerce were forgotten. The Dark Ages closed over most of Europe.

THE INFLUENCE OF ROME

With the Emperor gone, the Christian Bishop of Rome, the Pope, became the most important figure in Western Europe. His bishops and priests in every land looked to him for leadership as they tried to bring the peace and order of Roman ways to their unruly peoples. Roman learning and poetry were preserved because Latin continued to be the language of the Church. Roman customs, roads and buildings survived in many places. For centuries, Rome continued to spread a civilizing influence from the Imperial City.

PEOPLE AND EVENTS TO REMEMBER

753 B.C.	The founding of Rome
510	Kings turned out
396	Etruscan capital, Veii, taken
343–290	Conquest of Latin Tribes
272	Defeat of Pyrrhus
264–241	First War with Carthage
218–202	Hannibal fought against Rome
202	Battle of Zama
146	Destruction of Carthage
105–100	Marius consul
58–49	Julius Caesar in Gaul
44	Caesar murdered
31	Antony defeated at Actium
27	Augustus became first Emperor
*4	Birth of Jesus Christ

43 A.D.	Claudius added Britain to the Empire
46–52	St. Paul's journeys
54–68	Nero : persecution of Christians
98–117	Trajan
117–138	Hadrian
306–337	Constantine
313	Christianity became an official religion of the Empire
330	Constantine made Byzantium his capital
410	Goths sacked Rome
451	Attila and the Huns in Italy
476	Fall of the Roman Empire in the West

* Scholars now generally agree that Christ's birth occurred
4 years earlier than was believed

A magnificent Roman sculpture of two horses drawing a chariot. Even the chariot itself is intricately carved with a lion's head on the wheel-hub, and the long pole to which the horses are yoked ends in a beautifully carved ram's head

Olympia, where the first Olympic Games were held

17. WHAT WE OWE TO THE ANCIENT WORLD

It may seem in our present-day world of machinery, air travel and science, that the way people lived centuries ago has little meaning or importance. But if we stop to think, we shall find that the foundations of almost all that we do and believe in, lie in ancient times.

Since the rise of town-dwelling in Egypt and Sumeria, some 6,000 years ago, there has been an increasing knowledge and belief in the importance of good conduct, despite all the setbacks caused by innumerable wars and disasters.

Apart from power-driven machinery, the people of the Ancient World invented almost all the processes and arts of civilized living. Farming, building, road- and canal-making, trading methods, reading and writing all have developed from their beginnings in the Middle East. We owe many less important discoveries, such as the manufacture of clothes, pottery, furniture and even of central-heating, jewellery and ladies' make-up, to people who lived centuries before Christ.

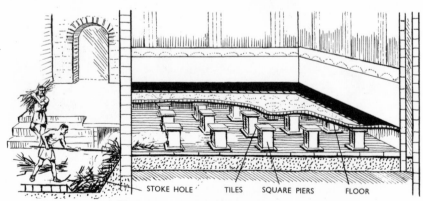

STOKE HOLE   TILES   SQUARE PIERS   FLOOR

A Hypocaust, or Roman central-heating system

The Parthenon of Athens, as it is today

The Greeks, more than any other people, gave us ideals and standards of beauty in sculpture, building and literature. They also founded the modern spirit of enquiry into the world we live in, through their discoveries in physics, mathematics, astronomy and medicine. Most important of all, perhaps, they showed us that good government depends upon the interest and effort of all citizens.

The Romans, less artistic but more practical, extended the Greek civilization, not so much by inventing as by improving on the ideas of others. They built better roads, bridges and aqueducts than any other people, and they understood big business and how to govern many lands with different peoples and religions. Above all, the Romans taught the importance of respect for law, and under their rule the Christian Church grew up. It is Christian teaching, together with the discoveries and ideas of the past, which is the basis of our present-day lives.

A Roman aqueduct

INDEX

930
U
UNSTEAD, ROBERT JOHN
    Looking at ancient history

	DATE DUE		
OCT 26	OCT 22 '90		
MAY 2 0	NOV 23 '90		
OCT 4	FAC		
NOV 19	FEB 10 1997		
FEB 25	Fac 99 00		
JUN 2			
SEP 30			
NOV 6			
MAR 2 9			
MAY 9			
JAN 6			
JAN 19			ALESCO